Africa Discovers Her Past

Africa Discovers Her Past

EDITED BY

J. D. FAGE

LONDON
OXFORD UNIVERSITY PRESS
IBADAN · NAIROBI
1970

Oxford University Press, Ely House, London W.1

GLASGOW NEW YORK TORONTO MELBOURNE WELLINGTON
CAPE TOWN SALISBURY IBADAN NAIROBI DAR ES SALAAM LUSAKA ADDIS ABABA
BOMBAY CALCUTTA MADRAS KARACHI LAHORE DACCA
KUALA LUMPUR SINGAPORE HONG KONG TOKYO

Printed in Great Britain by
Butler & Tanner Ltd, Frome and London

Foreword

THE ORIGINS of this little book lie in a series of broadcasts given in the B.B.C. African Service in 1967. It was thought that at least some of the matters discussed in these broadcasts were of sufficient general interest to merit their reappearance in book form. The Oxford University Press agreed to undertake the publication, and I was persuaded to act as editor.

Even though each contributor was asked to revise his original script for publication, the origin of the book in a series of talks broadcast over a considerable period of time is probably only too apparent. It has proved impossible to remove all the overlaps between one chapter and another which were probably inevitable in broadcasting, when quite a few listeners could not be expected to hear all the talks. However, some attempt has been made to provide cross-references.

There were also some gaps in the original scheme, and three entirely new chapters have therefore been commissioned by the publishers, from Professor Ogot on 'Historians and East Africa', from Dr Gray on 'Historians and Central Africa' and from Dr Birmingham on 'Historians and West Africa', to match the original contributions on North Africa and South Africa by Mr Atmore and Dr Marks.

Contents

CHAPTER ONE

Introduction

J. D. Fage

THE STUDY and teaching of the history of Africa is now a normal and respectable academic pursuit, not only in Africa itself, but also in universities in Britain and America, Poland and Russia, India and Brazil—indeed, throughout the world. But this has not always been so. The science or art of history as we know it was developed in western Europe as an outcome of its Renaissance of learning which began about the fourteenth century. This history was primarily concerned with tracing the development of the particular culture in which it had been born, the culture generally referred to as 'western civilization', from its origins in ancient Greece and Rome and Judaea. By the end of the eighteenth century, this culture had become a very successful and forceful culture, possessed of technological and economic strengths which enabled it to dominate the rest of the world.

Because of this, its historians gave scant attention to the culture and history of parts of the world outside Europe, whose peoples, so it was thought, had done far less to contribute to the general progress of mankind. Thus there is no treatment of Africa whatsoever in the first *Cambridge Modern History*, a great cooperative work which marked a high point of historical learning at the beginning of the present century. Twenty years later a distinguished British professor, A. P. Newton, a man very much concerned with the history of the world into which Europe had expanded, could actually say that Africa had *no* history before it was colonized by Europeans.

1

Of course this was nonsense. It is impossible for men to live together in any sort of a society without some recollection of its past, without some sense of its history. All sorts of things—for example marriage, inheritance, succession to office—cannot be regulated even in the smallest and simplest society if it has no rules, no customs, no history. It is true that extended families and small clan-groups do not need to maintain much record of their past beyond about three generations, say about a hundred years, a depth of time which would seem to provide a sufficient record for most of their needs. But one does not need to have much knowledge of African history to realize that for many centuries Negro Africans have been producing much more complex societies than mere extended families or clan-groups. Over two thousand years ago, there was the organized kingdom of Meroe in the upper Nile valley, while shortly after the Arabs established themselves in North Africa in the seventh century A.D., they recognized the existence, across the Sahara in West Africa, of such organized Negro kingdoms as ancient Ghana and Kanem. Kingdoms such as these, and many more, could not exist—could not regulate their internal affairs, could not deal with their neighbours, could not maintain their identities—without organized concepts of their history going back to the time of their foundation. At the time of the onset of European rule in Africa, there were quite a few African states which knew their history back for four or five or even more centuries.

There are still some western historians who maintain, regrettably, either that such histories cannot be properly studied, or that they are not worth studying. Among these is the present occupant of the Regius Chair of Modern History in the University of Oxford, Professor Hugh Trevor-Roper, some of whose opinions are quoted later in this book by Ivor Wilks. Professor Newton, incidentally, believed that there was no African history to study because, before the European colonization, the societies of Africa

2

were for the most part non-literate. 'History', he said, 'only begins when men take to writing.'

It is true that western historians, and hence historians in general, are accustomed to reconstructing the past largely from written evidence. But they do not depend on written evidence exclusively. Much of the history of Greece and Rome, and—increasingly—much of our knowledge of the early economic and social history of western Europe, is in fact based on the evidence of material remains which have been revealed and interpreted by archaeologists. Then, too, a fair amount of very recent history is apt to be based on oral sources. The importance of archaeology for African history is stressed in this book by Professors Shinnie and Thurstan Shaw, and of oral tradition by Professor Ryder.

But in any case, as Professor Wilks points out in his second contribution, Africa is not as devoid of written evidence for its pre-colonial history as Newton seems to have thought. It is true that most African peoples took to the idea of writing only rather recently, and that they borrowed it from Europeans, who had themselves borrowed it from the Semitic peoples. But some Semitic peoples live in Africa. North of the Sahara and in Ethiopia, writing is as old as, or older than, it is in western Europe. Writing in Arabic had spread south into West Africa long before this part of the continent was penetrated by Europeans. We know, as Professor Hunwick points out, of histories written in the western Sudan by African scholars at least as long ago as the sixteenth century. Then, too, a very considerable body of evidence of the African past has accumulated in the writings of men based outside Africa. Men are naturally curious, and they have been writing about Africa for a very long time, for at least two and a half thousand years. Herodotus, the Greek historian of the fifth century B.C., has quite a lot to say about Africa. So too have many other historians, geographers and travellers of ancient Greece and Rome and of medieval Islam, including, in the fourteenth century, Ibn Khaldun—and if Herodotus was

3

the 'father of history', Ibn Khaldun, a North African, seems to have been the first historian with the critical and analytical approach to his material that is demanded by the modern science. Then, too, there is a truly enormous amount of valuable material in the accounts and records of the growing host of western Europeans who became involved with Africa, at first mainly as explorers, traders and missionaries, from the fifteenth century onwards.

But it is only within the last twenty years or so that professional historians have appreciated the value of this great mass of written material as a source for the writing of the history of *Africa*. Since they were either westerners or western-trained, they originally looked at it with other purposes in mind: for the light that it shed on the classical or the Islamic worlds, or as material for the history of European expansion and colonialism. With Voltaire in the eighteenth century and Professor Trevor-Roper in our own time, they could not see that what had happened in Africa, what Africans themselves had done in the past, was of any value to the general history of mankind. The mainstream of human progress was Mediterranean and European; what had happened in Africa was, to quote Trevor-Roper, no more than 'the unrewarding gyrations of barbarous tribes'. Such African history as was written—by the nineteenth-century precursors of pan-Africanism, such as Edward Wilmot Blyden; by learned African clerics such as the nineteenth-century Ghanaian, Carl Christian Reindorf, or the Yoruba historian, Samuel Johnson; or by intelligent European administrators such as Maurice Delafosse or Harry Johnston—such African history was essentially the work of gifted and dedicated amateurs who were not recognized by the professional historians, and whose work was little regarded in the universities or in the schools, whether within or without Africa.[1]

Since 1948, however, there has been a total revolution in African historiography. That year marked the effective

[1] See Chapter Two.

beginning of the modern movement which has led to the establishment of universities throughout tropical Africa. For the first time, professional historians began to work in Africa, and they did so in ever-increasing numbers. If initially most of them were Europeans, their students were Africans in Africa, and part of their duty was to train African historians. In this context, the old Europa-centric view of history could be maintained no longer.

By an interesting coincidence, events in Ghana in that same year, 1948, were to provide the first steps in what became the rapid march of the erstwhile African colonies to independent nationhood. It thus became urgently necessary to explore and to make known the historical heritage of these new nations, to establish their roots, not only as a reaction to the colonial situation, but also in the whole stream of the African past. The written sources, including the records of the colonial era, needed to be reassessed in African terms. Means had to be sought to fill in the gaps left by the written sources.

Many techniques and disciplines have been enlisted in the search to recover the history of Africa: archaeology, comparative linguistics, even such obscure subjects as ethno-botany. But the professional historians, African and non-African, who were now available for the task were naturally most interested in historical records. One of the most significant results of their work of the last twenty years has been the appreciation of the value of oral records. The African societies which existed on the eve of the colonial period, including such major states as Ashanti and Benin, Buganda and Bunyoro, could not be maintained without elaborate records of their foundation, records of the succession to the kingship and to other offices, of the rules of law and of land tenure, of their relations with neighbouring societies, and of many other things besides. If they were unable to maintain these things in writing, they had to devise formal and regular means of passing them on by word of mouth. They had in fact to have their regular chroniclers or archivists, men whose duty it was to maintain the official record and to transmit it intact to their heirs and successors.

There are many problems involved in the proper understanding and use of these formal oral traditions.[2] They can, for instance, be incomplete or corrupt (whether by accident or by intention), and one must always remember that they represent the past as the rulers need it to be remembered. Oral tradition may not always tell the truth—but then, no more do written documents. The truth is always something that the historian must seek out, that he must approach by the analysis and comparison of the sources available to him. In many African societies, he is greatly helped by their possession of oral records. They enable him to clothe the rather bare framework provided by the largely external written sources, while on the other hand the latter provide a useful perspective in which to set the oral evidence. When put together with the other evidence, that from archaeology, linguistics and anthropology, as well as that from the written sources, the oral records often help the historian to reconstruct the history of Africa as successfully and as fruitfully as the history of almost any other part of the world.

[2] See Chapters Two and Five.

CHAPTER TWO

African Historiographical Traditions, Old and New

Ivor Wilks

ALMOST A century and a half ago, in his lectures on the philosophy of history, Hegel advanced the view that Africa 'is no historical part of the World; it has no movement or development to exhibit'. Only a few years ago the Regius Professor of History in the University of Oxford created something of a furore among Africanists by reviving this view. 'There is', he observed of the African past, 'only the unrewarding gyrations of barbarous tribes in picturesque but irrelevant corners of the globe.' Professors Hegel and Trevor-Roper stand, in time, at the beginning and end of a period during which most of those concerned with the history of the African continent laboured under the influence of a myth of white superiority. Missionaries, travellers, administrators and soldiers, usually European but sometimes African, delved into the past of the societies in which they found themselves, and recorded the results of their inquiries. All however worked to some degree or other under the aegis of an imperial government and within a framework of Christian belief. Their interpretations of what they found tended accordingly to reflect official and often racialist attitudes. Binger, to whom we are indebted for much valuable historical information, exemplifies well the outlook of the time. Visiting the Mossi capital of Wagadugu in 1888, he commented:

if the European should ever come here, he should come as master, constituting the high class of society, and should not

7

have to bow his head before indigenous chiefs, to whom he is infinitely superior in all respects.[1]

Binger was a Frenchman. His contemporary, Carl Christian Reindorf, was a Gold Coast African who in 1895 wrote a *History of the Gold Coast and Asante* which is still widely read and which is meritorious in many respects. But Reindorf ended his book with a poem:

> Rule, supremely rule, Britannia, rule,
> Thy newly acquired Colony on the Gold Coast! . . .
> Two mighty foes impede her way,
> Ignorance and blood-stained superstition.
> To rule and not to fight such deadly foes,
> Is not Britannia's way. . . .

The metre may be obscure, but the sentiment is clear enough.

Writers within this tradition not unexpectedly came to see the colonial era as essentially an Age of Enlightenment. As a result, quite different terminologies came to be used according to whether that, or the preceding period, was being described. Thus what was referred to as 'government' in the colonial situation was categorized as 'despotism' in the pre-colonial, and colonial 'taxation' was therefore pre-colonial 'extortion'. Anything classed as a 'military expedition' or 'police action' in the colonial period was almost inevitably stigmatized as a 'slave raid' in an earlier time. Presented in such terms, African history was used to justify the imposition of colonial regimes upon the indigenous political systems: it became incumbent upon the imperial powers to halt slave-raiding and to free the people from the tyranny of their rulers and the rapacity of their officials. Most sensationalistic and frequently used of all such devices, however, was that of describing judicial executions as 'human sacrifices'. Ashanti, for example, was a West African state which in the nineteenth century

[1] L. G. Binger, *Du Niger au Golfe de Guinée* (Paris, 1892), Vol. 1, p. 467.

had come to approximate closely to the typical European nation-state, and which had offered particularly strong resistance to imperial encroachment. It is thus especially significant that successive writers in that century increasingly fostered an image of Ashanti as the land of 'human sacrificers'—as Bramston of the Colonial Office put it in 1895 when he refused even to receive an Ashanti embassy which had arrived in London. Yet a critical examination of the sources suggests that a kingdom such as Ashanti was much too concerned with the conservation of its man-power resources lightly to dissipate these by mass sacrifices; though Ashanti, like most European countries at the time, executed its criminals or rebels publicly—usually on state occasions, when the maximum deterrent effect would be exercised upon the assembled citizenry. But beliefs die hard: in 1954 a reputable European historian could still comment that in Ashanti 'the amount of torture and human sacrifice for ritualistic purposes exceeded even the wildest imaginations of the most hardened Europeans'.

The decolonization of African history is a process that has been gathering momentum over the last two decades. Broadly, it has involved the treatment of African societies as ones concerned with the pursuit of rationally thought-out ends by rationally conceived means. Already new appraisals of the extraordinarily complex political systems of the so-called African 'despotisms' have been made, while the aims, for example, of a West African nineteenth-century resistance leader such as the *Almamy* Samori Toure, so long dismissed by historians as no more than a slave-raider, have been shown to include a major commitment to social reform. The decolonization process has been greatly advanced by the application of the most recent standards and techniques of historical scholarship to the elucidation of the African past. This has been made possible by the enormous growth in the number of professional historians supported both by the new African universities and by the many centres of African Studies which have emerged elsewhere. The decolonization process has been stimulated, however, by the influence of a tradition of African historiography which had developed earlier than, and therefore independently of, that of the colonial writers. The origins of this tradition lie far back in the African past, and its roots deep within African society.

A characteristic feature of many pre-literate societies of tropical Africa is what may be described as the *continuous application* of the past to matters of everyday life. The living generation regards itself as essentially the link between the dead ancestors and those yet unborn. While in England, for example, comparatively few people could name even their paternal great-grandparent (at least without having researched the topic), in many African communities it is common for an individual to be able to recite the names of his ancestors for upwards of five generations, recounting where each had lived and died, in which wars he may have fought, what land he may have acquired, and which women he married and from where. Frequently the affairs of government are conducted with reference to memorized narratives transmitted verbally from generation to generation. Often the recitation of these oral 'texts' is the task of trained specialists such as the famous *griots* of the western Sudan, or the *kwadwom* singers of Ashanti.

Sometimes the texts are cast in fable form, like the well-known Ananse stories which survive in the Caribbean as well as in West Africa. More usually, however, they have an historical form. A family may legitimate its claims to a certain political office by recounting the historical circumstances of the original grant: for example, how their ancestor fought well in a specified war and was rewarded by being given such-and-such an office. Similarly the territorial boundaries between two communities will be defined with reference to a putatively historic agreement between two early hunters or warriors who met at a certain hill or river. Sometimes of course the accounts thus given are clearly not factual—as with groups which claim allodial rights over a given tract of land by asserting that their ancestors 'came out of a hole in the ground there', or 'descended there by a chain from the sky'. More usually however the accounts look factual enough, and sometimes it is possible to test their veracity against independent but contemporary documentary sources—for example, the reports of traders or missionaries. It is remarkable how often a knowledge of events that occurred even three or four centuries ago has been accurately transmitted in these oral narratives.

Pre-literate African societies, then, show a major concern with matters historical: the past is of crucial relevance to their very existence, and is not merely of speculative interest. The necessary condition for the emergence of an historiographical tradition is, in other words, present in such societies. A sufficient condition must be the appearance within them of a literate class. In parts of both East and West Africa this condition was satisfied as a result of the spread of Islam and, with this, a knowledge of the Arabic script and language. The development of the Indian Ocean trade between the Arabian peninsula and the East African coast, and of the trans-Saharan trade between North Africa and the western Sudan, led to the Islamization of local societies in both regions, to the increasing use of Arabic as the language of a growing educated class, and ultimately to the appearance of written histories.

The author of the earliest known East African history, *Kitab al-Sulwa fi akhbar Kulwa*, 'The Book of Consolation of the History of Kilwa', was born in 1499 and started writing probably around 1520 or 1530. The work is a history of the trading town of Kilwa from the time of its supposed foundation in the tenth century, and the author was commissioned to write it by the reigning Sultan, Muhammad b. al-Husayn. The earliest known historical work of

West African authorship dates from the same period. It is the *Ta'rikh Al-Fattash*, 'History of the Searcher', commenced in 1519 by Mahmud Ka'ti of Timbuctu, and subsequently enlarged and edited by one of his grandsons. It is essentially an account of the reigns of the Songhai kings of that region, about whom the author recounts many entertaining stories, but also includes much information on the Muslim scholars of the town. Both these Kilwa and Timbuctu works are highly sophisticated enterprises by the standards of the time, whether Muslim or Christian, and it is difficult to believe that they represent the very beginnings of the historiographical tradition in their respective localities. It is still possible that earlier works will come to light.

Because of the failure of Islam to influence areas beyond the coast and its immediate hinterland in East Africa, the tradition there remained a restricted one. Works are still being found, however, like the *Kitab al-Zunuj*, 'The Book of Zanj', which is a late-nineteenth-century compilation of earlier written sources, and the Chronicles of Pate and Lamu which were composed in the Swahili language. In West Africa, by contrast, historical writing rapidly acquired a considerable vogue, although many works have undoubtedly been lost in the course of time. A younger contemporary of Mahmud Ka'ti, writing independently in Bornu, was its chief *Imam*, Ahmad ibn Fartuwa, who in the later part of the sixteenth century produced several works on the history of that kingdom, probably at the request of the reigning *Mai*, Idris Alooma. In the next century, again in Timbuctu, 'Abd al-Rahman al-Sa'di put together between 1629 and 1655 his famous *Ta'rikh al-Sudan*, 'History of the [Western] Sudan', while in the middle of the same century a writer in the Hausa city of Kano produced the *'Asl al-Wanghariyin*, 'Origins of the Wangara', in which he gives an account of the arrival there of Malian immigrants in the latter part of the fifteenth century. It is interesting to note that this work is prefaced by a section on the Wangara homeland on the Upper Niger; it is based upon a twelfth-century account of it by the Sicilian Arab geographer al-Idrisi, whose writings must therefore have been known in seventeenth-century Kano.

By the eighteenth century, local histories in Arabic were being produced in parts of West Africa far distant from the greater Islamic centres like Timbuctu or Kano. In the second decade of that century, for example, a Muslim scholar committed to writing from oral narratives a series of stories about the early history of the Gonja state, which lies only just north of the forest zone of what is now Ghana. These were typical examples of what is called in Arabic *khabar*, concise accounts of single events—the arrival in Gonja of the founder of the ruling dynasty; the conversion of the rulers to Islam. Subsequently some of these fragments were utilized as the opening sections of a more ambitious work, the *Kitab Ghunja*, 'Book of Gonja', written in 1751/2 by al-Hajj Muhammad ibn al-Mustafa, member of a Gonja family which supplied *Imams* and other Muslim functionaries to the rulers. The *Kitab Ghunja*, however, also includes annals of local occurrences arranged chronologically: of wars, famines, deaths and the like. It was subsequently updated to 1765 by another member of the same family, and continues to be read and re-copied to this day in Gonja; a number of extensive glosses on it, and even radically revised editions of it, have been produced by Gonja scholars in this century.

There are now few Muslim communities of any size in West Africa which do not possess locally written histories, though many works were lost in the wars of the late nineteenth century when resistance leaders like Samori pursued a scorched-earth policy in an attempt to halt the advance of the European military columns. Much nevertheless survives. In the small town of Wa in north-western Ghana, for example, I have been able to examine a score of works in Arabic script, and in both Arabic and Hausa languages, which are historical in content. Some are only a folio or two in length, others more substantial. The earliest appears to date from the beginning of the nineteenth century. Most treat of the origins of the Wa state in the late seventeenth and early eighteenth centuries, and of the agreements made between the ethnically diverse groups which contracted to join together at that time. These texts are still frequently referred to in the resolution of constitutional disputes within the traditional body politic, and are made readily available for consultation.

Sometimes, however, an historical work may become withdrawn from the public domain and may acquire an almost magical significance. A short Arabic work entitled *Isnad al-Sudan*, 'The Chain of Tradition of the Sudan', is clearly ancient and has been so often re-copied that the accretion of scribal errors over the centuries has made the only text I have seen quite incomprehensible. The work, which is in the possession of a Malinke-Dyula family in the Ivory Coast, has an official custodian. When a custodian dies, a ring is stirred into a pot of rice and whoever receives it in his portion then assumes charge of the manuscript. Since a custodian thus chosen may be illiterate in Arabic, a scholar is also appointed as 'secretary' to the text, and he appears to use it in fact as a mnemonic device for a long narrative account of a series of wars in the old Mali empire, which led to the dispersion of various Malinke groups from their homeland. Such a case does represent an advanced state of decay in the historiographical tradition: it is but one stage from reversion to oral tradition. To write history is essentially to bring it into the public domain, where it is open to inspection and criticism; oral tradition is by contrast a form of private property, belonging to this or that dynasty, lineage or family. But the example of *Isnad al-Sudan* is exceptional. Most historians in West Africa recognize that the obligation of publication is generated by the act of writing, and therefore readily allow their works to be copied and distributed.

In this century the old West African historiographical

tradition has continued to flourish, and works like those of
the Wazir of Sokoto, Junaida, on Hausaland; Shaykh Musa
Kamara on Senegal; Ahmad ibn Abi Bakr on northern
Yorubaland; or Mahmud ibn ʿAbdallah on Gonja may be
paralleled in many other areas. The lengthy history of
Massina by Amadu Hampaté Ba and J. Daget, although
written in French and printed in 1962, belongs essentially
to this same tradition. The vigour and versatility of these
writers is well exemplified in al-Hajj Muhammad Marhaba
Saghanughu, *Mufti* of Bobo-Dioulasso in the Ivory Coast.
Author in his own right of numerous works on the Islamization process in West Africa, al-Hajj Muhammad has
also greatly stimulated local historical studies by his new
editions of earlier and largely unknown texts which he has
located in the libraries of the ʿulama. These include works
on the Diakhanke of Futa Jalon in Guinea, on the Watara
of Kong in the Ivory Coast, on the Mossi of Wagadugu in
Upper Volta, and on the *jihad* of al-Hajj Mahmud Karan-
taw. The strength of the writers who lie in this tradition,
running from Mahmud Kaʿti in the sixteenth century to,
say, al-Hajj Muhammad Saghanughu in this, is in their
privileged access to local knowledge and in their acquaintance with (if not always participation in) the value-systems
of those about whom they wrote.

ʿAbd al-Rahman al-Saʿdi's characterization of history in
the seventeenth century sounds familiar enough to modern
ears:

the science is rich in jewels and fertile in information, since it
makes man understand his country, his ancestors, its annals,
the names of great men and their lives,

and there was perhaps little to choose, in terms of standards
of scholarship, between the leading West African writers
of that century and their European counterparts. Subsequently, however, developments in the European tradition
found no parallel in the African one: while the former
became increasingly analytical and thematic, the latter

remained firmly narrative and annalistic; while the former concerned itself increasingly with social and economic issues, the latter continued to be political and biographical. Nevertheless, in the nineteenth century the two traditions did come together at points. Early in the century, for example, Joseph Dupuis visited Kumasi as consular agent of the British government, and, by virtue of his knowledge of Arabic, was able to establish close relations with the leaders of the Muslim community there. From them he obtained an account of the rise of Ashanti, with chronologies, which he later incorporated into his *Journal of a Residence in Ashantee*, published in 1824. This was one of the earliest historical accounts of the Ashanti kingdom to be published, and successive writers in the European tradition have continued to the present to treat its history within the chronological and conceptual framework derived from the Kumasi Muslims.

It was however with the publication of Henry Barth's monumental *Travels and Discoveries in North and Central Africa* in 1857–58, which included excerpts from the writings of the Western Sudanese scholars, that European historians were for the first time in a position to appreciate the richness of the African works. In 1898 and 1900 an Arabic text and French translation of the *Ta'rikh al-Sudan* were published in Paris, to be followed a decade and a half later by those of the *Ta'rikh al-Fattash*. About this time, too, in the then French West African territories, a series of remarkable men such as Charles Monteil and Maurice Delafosse associated themselves with the Muslim scholars, and out of this experience produced a number of works which opened up the possibilities of unlimited research. In the former British territories one comparable figure towers above his contemporaries, that of Sir Richmond Palmer, who steeped himself in the writings of the historians of Hausaland and Bornu and produced a series of translations of their works into English. Yet the labours of Monteil, Delafosse, Palmer and others in this period produced singularly little response: the historians of Africa of the time were working, as we have seen, with a set of presuppositions that effectively prevented any close *rapprochement* between them and the West African Muslim writers.

There was a time when the history of European activities in Africa could be regarded, *pace* Hegel, as the only valid kind of African history. Today the former is seen as but one aspect of the latter. Likewise, until recently the works of historians trained in the European tradition have been taken to represent the mainstream of African historiography—and the writings of the Muslim scholars have been considered, at best, as 'source material'. It may be that the process of the decolonization of African history will involve, first, the purging of the works of the colonial historians of their more bizarre interpretations; second, the integration of this more recent tradition with the older one; and third, the application of the most rigorous standards and techniques of scholarship to a unified tradition.

CHAPTER THREE

Archaeology and African History

P. L. Shinnie

OVER A great deal of the African continent there was no writing before the Arabs or the Europeans came, and therefore man was not able to leave documents describing life in the past. So when we want to discover the past history of Africa, the way man lived, and the comings and goings of different peoples, we have no such information as existed, for example, for the ancient world of the Mediterranean, where many written documents and inscriptions have helped us to understand the past.

Of course some parts of Africa had writing, and in Egypt we have some of the oldest written documents in the world. As a result of this we know a great deal more about Ancient Egypt than we do of other parts of the continent, and we can trace its history for about five thousand years. But for most of the African continent, and for all that part which lies south of the Sudan, there is little or no writing, and we have to use other methods if we are to understand what went on in past centuries and if we are to produce an account of past human activity.

Without documents there are many things we cannot know, but increasingly a broad picture of the past and a knowledge of how man lived and what objects he used can be got by the study of archaeology. Of all the new methods now being used to investigate the story of pre-literate societies, archaeology is probably the one that will tell us the most. Archaeology is the study of the material remains left by man in the past. It covers all periods of human history, and its aim is to examine everything which has survived from the past; whether it is the remains of man himself, his skeleton—which tells us something of what sort of man he was; or the remains of the things he used—his pots, his tools and weapons, whatever they may have been made of; or the remains of his houses or huts, and anything else that may have survived from the past. Many people think of archaeologists as being only concerned with excavation, that is digging up the remains of earlier man from the soil in which the years have buried them. Excavation is a very important part of archaeology and, in Africa, where it is a comparatively new study, where so much needs to be found out, and where as yet there are no big collections of material, it is of special importance, and archaeologists must spend much of their time digging. But there are other ways in which archaeology can be carried out, both in the field and in the museum. Many scholars travel the countryside searching for sites of ancient occupation and marking them on maps for future excavation or study, whilst others examine the objects found by excavators and subject them to minute and careful examination in the study and the laboratory, trying to understand what these objects can tell us of the past.

But the main work is excavation, and this requires skill and care if the fullest information is to be obtained. Unfortunately the environment over much of Africa is unfavourable to the preservation of many of the things that past men made and used. Egypt is exceptionally good for preservation: its dry climate has meant that all sorts of objects have been found, so that in addition to what we can learn from Egypt's written records, we have very detailed information on many aspects of Egyptian life. Further south conditions are not so good. In the region of the Sudan, immediately south of Egypt, the white ant—or termite—is a great enemy of the archaeologist, and eats many of the objects made of organic matter, such as wood, cloth, leather, basketry and so on. Further south again, and also in West Africa, the very damp climate and the acid in the soil tend to destroy organic materials. So in many parts of Africa the archaeologist has to reconstruct the past from objects of pottery and stone, both of which resist white ants and damp weather. Sometimes metal survives, though metal too, particularly iron, is vulnerable to damp climates, and rusts away. So the archaeologist's work is not easy—he needs skill and experience in digging, so that the evidence does not get destroyed in the act of being dug out, and so that the maximum information can be obtained from what are often only very partial remains; and he needs patience in studying the objects afterwards.

If the archaeologist in Africa wants to make the greatest contribution to the unravelling of the continent's history, he must choose the places in which he works with great care, asking himself before he starts what historical questions need an answer. One of the questions that is always asked of archaeologists by the public is 'How do you know where to dig?', and this question deserves a careful answer. The archaeologist does not just blindly drive his pick into the ground, or go to a place where legend says treasure is to be found—for it is not treasure he is looking for, but information. Before he starts his work the archaeologist must have a good and detailed knowledge of the country or area in which he is going to operate. He must know about the people and the geography of modern times, as he must know of the past. And of the past he must have studied all the available information, so as to know what the main gaps in knowledge are, and to be able to judge where archaeology can help. Often traditional stories will lead him to places which were inhabited in past days; or personal observation of mounds, ditches and other earthworks or signs of disturbance of the surface of the earth in earlier times may reveal centres of ancient importance.

Perhaps some examples from my own experience will show this more clearly. Some years ago I was working in Uganda, where one of the most interesting problems is the understanding of the past history of the states of the Bantu-speaking peoples, Buganda, Bunyoro and others, which seem to have developed, if the traditions are right, in the region north of Lake Victoria in the sixteenth century. Over a wide area of south-western Uganda are a number of large earthwork enclosures, formed by elaborate arrangements of ditches cut into the earth. These enclosures, many of them very big, are said to have been made by a people known as the Bacwezi, the semi-mythical founders of the kingdoms. Nothing was known of these people other than what the oral traditions had to say, and, as often is the case, these were difficult to interpret. So here seemed a suitable subject for archaeological investigation, and the most famous of these sites, Bigo, on the Katonga River in western Buganda, was selected for excavation. Three seasons of digging have now been carried out there, firstly by myself and later by Professor Merrick Posnansky, and, though not all the results have yet been published, we now have considerable information about the material culture of the inhabitants of Bigo. We know what their pottery was like (and can therefore identify other sites where similar pottery is found as having been inhabited by the same people), we know something of their iron weapons, and we can see from the massive ditches dug and mounds raised that there must have been a considerable amount of social organization and discipline. The layout of the very complex arrangements of ditches confirms the traditional evidence that Bigo was an important centre, perhaps the capital, of the Bacwezi.

Let me take another example from my work, this time in West Africa. Some years ago it was thought that attention should be turned to northern Ghana, and in particular to the area known as Dagomba, where the kingdom of that name had existed from the early fifteenth century. The outline of the history of the region was known from the lists of kings remembered by special officials of the court of the Ya Na, as the king of Dagomba is called. The names of rulers and the length of their reigns were known, as well as the main incidents of each reign, so it was possible to fix dates for many of these incidents, and even to know approximately the time at which the Dagomba state was founded. What we were ignorant of was the material culture of early Dagomba, nor was it possible to attribute any date to the small number of antiquities, mainly pottery, already found, mostly by chance, in northern Ghana. Fortunately local tradition remembered the site of an early Dagomba town, a place now known as Yendi Dabari, which had been the capital at an earlier date. Not only was the site of the now abandoned and deserted town known, but even the dates at which it was occupied could be approximately fixed. It was said to have been founded in about 1500 and to have remained occupied until about 1640, when it was abandoned under military pressure from the west, and the capital was moved further east to its present site at Yendi. Archaeological excavation could therefore do two things: firstly, it could show something of what an early Dagomba town was like, and what sort of things the people used; and secondly, if a firm date could be given to objects found there, particularly the pottery, it would make it possible to date similar objects found in other parts of northern Ghana. Since fashion in pottery changes from time to time, it could be assumed that pieces of pottery found in other places that resembled those found in the excavations at Yendi Dabari were of about the same date.

First examination of the site, now in thick bush, showed a number of mounds which looked like the ruins of round huts of earth of the type still in use in Dagomba. But excavation of some of these mounds, after a massive operation to clear the bush, gave a rather different and very interesting picture of what at least part of the old town had looked like. Instead of the round huts we had expected, we found a large rectangular building of many rooms, and with some evidence to suggest that it had been of two stories. In addition to this building, and close to it, was a large open courtyard paved with the local laterite gravel, and surrounded by an earth wall. This was certainly not what had been expected.

To understand fully the significance of these remains, more excavation must be carried out; perhaps the typical Dagomba huts are waiting to be found in another part of the site still covered by bush. But what our work did show was that large buildings were in use, and that some activity necessitated a large enclosed area. The most likely solution of this puzzle is that by chance we had stumbled on an area occupied by traders from the north, where rectangular and many-storied buildings were common, and that the courtyard was required for the safe keeping, and the loading and unloading of the caravans of animals that the northern traders brought with them. The objects found in the excavation were not very exciting, rather dull and plain pottery, but it is useful to know what the pottery was like at this date, and there were some metal implements, and clay tobacco pipes. The latter are important as dating evidence, as they cannot have been made or used before tobacco was introduced after the discovery of America by Columbus.

Both these two sites of which I have spoken, one in East and one in West Africa, may have been of some importance in adding to our knowledge of the past, but they did not produce any objects of artistic merit. But this is not because such objects have not been found in Africa. At Ife, in Nigeria, a splendid series of sculptured heads have been found, some in bronze and some in terra cotta, i.e. baked clay. These remarkable examples of African art have been known for many years, but there has been very little knowledge as to the date at which they were made or the reasons which caused the artists of Ife to produce such beautiful objects. During the last ten years there has been much archaeological investigation at Ife in an attempt to answer some of these questions, and particularly to try to establish the dates at which they were produced and to see how old the earliest ones are. By a long and detailed study of Ife and its art, Professor Frank Willett was able to suggest that the earliest sculptures might go back at least to the fourteenth century, but this dating was arrived at more by studying the oral traditions and the artistic development than by strictly archaeological means. In spite of years of highly skilled and careful excavation, during which many new pieces of sculpture were found, for long nothing was discovered to establish a firm dating. These rather negative results from Ife demonstrate one of the great difficulties which face the archaeologist working in Africa when he is trying to date the objects he has found.[1]

Over a great deal of the world archaeology has been going on so long, and so much has been done, that the objects found are usually too well known for dating them to present much difficulty. For literate periods they can often be identified with quite short periods of time and even with known events. In Africa this is not so, and since a pot or a piece of sculpture does not in itself bear evidence of date, its age can only be told in a limited number of ways. Firstly, it can be dated if it is found associated with objects whose date is known from other information, and for West Africa during the comparatively recent period from which I have drawn my examples, this normally means European imports. Secondly, oral tradition, if sufficiently precise, as at Yendi Dabari, can give a date. Thirdly, if there is organic material, laboratory tests to discover how much of the radioactive material Carbon-14 is left can give a date[2]—but as has already been said, in many parts of Africa little of this type of material survives.

[1] This chapter was originally prepared in 1967, when Professor Willett's methods of dating were those described in his book *Ife in the History of West African Sculpture*, which was published in that year. Since then, however, Professor Willett has received radiocarbon dates for material he excavated at Ife. These are published in his chapter in J. D. Fage and Roland Oliver, *Papers in African Prehistory* (1969), and suggest that the history of Ife sculpture must certainly go back to about the eleventh century. (For radiocarbon dating, see Chapter Four.)

[2] See Chapter Four.

In Ife, no foreign imports were found, nor, until recently, was there any material available for Carbon-14 dating; so only oral tradition, the least precise of these methods, could be of help and give an approximate date. But even this approximation was a great advance on previous knowledge, and we knew far more of Ife, its history, and the artistic development there over the last few hundred years than we did before the archaeologist went to work.

So bit by bit, often slowly and painfully, the archaeologist adds his share to our knowledge of Africa's history. Often it seems that he is dealing with matters of small importance, and a piece of pottery or a tool of stone may not seem an object of great significance on which to develop ideas and theories of man's history. But from such objects, the real things those men used in the past, we know that we can, in time, understand how those men lived.

CHAPTER FOUR

Archaeology and the Dating of the African Past

Thurstan Shaw

IN TRYING to trace the story of what happened in the long history of Africa's past, one of the difficulties is to say just *when* different events took place. Where there are no written records to give us dates, we have to devise other means of dating the various things that we know took place. The methods we use for this in Africa are fundamentally the same as the methods of archaeological dating used all over the world.

What are these methods? They divide themselves roughly into two kinds: *relative* dating, and *absolute* dating. Let us first consider relative dating, which for many years was the only form of dating available to archaeologists dealing with the remains of societies with no writing.

The principle of relative dating is fairly obvious—you can say that event A took place before event B, which in turn took place before C—but you may not be able to say within two or three centuries how many years B.C. or A.D. any one of them took place.

If you have two successive sets of people living in a cave, in which their food remains, lost tools and general occupational rubbish accumulate, it is common sense that the remains of the later people will be at the top, those of the earlier at the bottom. If on a number of sites in a given area you always find one type of material lying above another, it is fair to say that the upper succeeded the lower in time. In sub-Saharan Africa we always find the introduction of iron succeeding the use of stone and bone for tools and weapons.

Similarly, if you find the remains of a building set on a level above the remains of other walls or floors, it is fair to presume that the latter are older. It is also sometimes possible to see, with adjacent buildings on the same level, that one must have been built before another—as in the case of some of the pyramids at Meroe in the Sudan. The same kind of inferences have been drawn in studying the different parts of the stone walls of Zimbabwe, in Rhodesia, to establish a relative time-scale for different ruins and different building periods.

The same principle can be applied to engravings and paintings on rock surfaces, which are common in many parts of Africa. Such rock paintings are notoriously difficult to date in absolute terms, yet it may nevertheless be possible to observe that one particular style of painting or colouring, or one particular subject-matter, always underlies another—and from this, useful conclusions about their relative ages may be drawn.

Objects such as tools and weapons made by man change with time, either in response to changes in the environment, or as the result of human inventiveness; objects of art and decoration also change with time, partly for the same reasons, partly as the result of social change, or simply as the result of changes in fashion and taste. Such changes in form give rise to the study of types, known as typology. When a sequence of such typological changes has been established by archaeological methods, and a relative dating for the different types has been securely confirmed by stratigraphy, it may be possible to use typology alone for dating purposes. If I found a specimen of the stone tool known to archaeologists as an Acheulian cleaver, I could say with some degree of confidence that it was a lot older than the type known as a microlith. But this is only because the relative ages of such objects have been established on hundreds of sites and without any exceptions. It is dangerous to use typology for dating purposes where the stratigraphy of the typological sequence has *not* been demonstrated, or to construct a time-sequence from typology alone.

In areas which have no written dates themselves, but which are adjacent to or were trading with an area which has, it may be possible to obtain approximate datings relative to the dated area. In the Middle East written dates can take us back about five thousand years, but most of Mediterranean Europe does not have written dates until about two thousand years later, and most of northern Europe not for a further thousand years. Yet during this period of three thousand years, useful dating evidence is obtained from objects imported into Europe from the Middle East.

This method can be useful in African archaeology too. On the East African coast, on the sites of the medieval trading stations, are found pieces of Chinese porcelain; as the dates of the various kinds of porcelain found are known, this helps to give some idea of the dates of the East African sites. I said 'some idea' advisedly, because you have to be careful how you use this type of dating evidence. You can only really use it as a 'limit after which' your material must be dated—that is, your site producing imported Chinese porcelain *cannot* be earlier than the known date of that type of porcelain, but *could* be later—perhaps very much later.

In Ghana I once excavated a large mound, twenty-five feet high, in the top half of which there were many locally made clay smoking pipes, while in the bottom half there were none. Now we know that the habit of tobacco-smoking was introduced to Europe from America during the sixteenth century, and that it spread around the world during the seventeenth; there is plenty of evidence for this. The level in the mound in Ghana at which tobacco pipes first occur could not be earlier than A.D. 1600, and in fact was probably not much before A.D. 1650.

Glass beads manufactured outside Africa are frequently encountered on African archaeological sites, and if only we knew with certainty what types of beads were manufactured in India, Arab Egypt and Venice at different periods, they might help us a lot with our dating problems. But we do not yet have this knowledge, and the whole matter is very complex; some styles of beads may remain popular for centuries, and some may be treasured as heirlooms or as insignia for generations.

Now let us turn our attention to the so-called 'absolute' methods of archaeological dating. These methods are called 'absolute' only because they deal in numbers of years before the present; they are not absolute in the sense of being 'absolutely accurate'. Thus they are not *historical* dates; in fact most of them are only estimated.

The best known of these methods is that of radiocarbon dating. An isotope of carbon is produced in the upper atmosphere with fourteen particles in the nucleus instead of the usual twelve. Together with normal carbon it is taken into the system of everything living. However Carbon-14 is unstable, and decays with a half-life of about 5,700 years. As soon as anything dies, the proportion of Carbon-14 to Carbon-12 begins to fall. In dead organic matter, therefore, it is possible to estimate how long has elapsed since the moment of death, by measuring the proportion of Carbon-14 surviving against the amount of Carbon-12. Bone, wood, charcoal and shell can all be dated in this way. But, just as it is possible to say what is the *average* length of life of human beings, although a knowledge of the average does not enable you to predict how long any one individual will live, so a statement of the half-life of Carbon-14 is an *average*, and in each case there is a given range of error. Because radiocarbon dating is a calculation of this sort, Carbon-14 ages are always given with a plus-or-minus figure after them, indicating one standard error. Thus if a date is given as 1,000 ± 100 years before the present, it means that there are two chances in three that the actual date lies between 900 and 1,100 years ago; there is still one chance in three that it lies outside these limits, although only one chance in twenty that it lies outside the range 800 to 1,200 years ago.

Now you might say that a date as vague as that is not much use, especially as there are other possible sources of error in radiocarbon dating as well; in a way this is true for a *single* radiocarbon age determination. However, it has been found that where you have blocks and constellations of radiocarbon dates all telling the same story, there is no good reason to doubt the information they give; and in the circumstances of African archaeology, they may be the *only* indications of date it is possible to obtain. Radiocarbon dating has in the last fifteen years revolutionized the prehistoric archaeology of Europe and south-west Asia, and now at last it is providing us with a tool to establish a chronological framework for the prehistoric cultures of Africa.

Radiocarbon dating is not of much service for periods earlier than forty thousand years ago, but for these remoter periods there are other methods of dating similarly dependent on radioactive breakdown, such as the uranium/thorium and potassium/argon methods. These are valuable in providing absolute dating in the earliest period of man's development, for the history of which Africa is the most important continent in the world; for the dating of this period we are otherwise dependent upon relative dating methods arising from geological data, and evidence derived from changes in flora, fauna and climate. The study of fossil pollen, for example, can indicate not only past climatic changes, but can also show up human interference with the natural environment, such as occurs with the introduction of agriculture. This study of fossil pollen has been a highly successful instrument of relative dating in temperate zones, but is still awaiting development in the tropics.

A new method of determining the age of pottery—known

as 'thermoluminescent dating', and again dependent on physics—is being worked on, and, if successful, holds out great hope for obtaining dates in all the later African cultures.

Naturally the best results for dating the African past are obtained when as many methods as possible can be used, both relative and absolute, for dating archaeological sites and finds. A few radiocarbon dates injected into a strati-graphically established sequence of cultures will give it entirely new meaning and significance. A combination of careful and skilful observation of stratigraphy with a limited number of radiocarbon dates has in the last ten years revolutionized our knowledge of the Zimbabwe ruins in Rhodesia and of their stages of development. Reliable typologies, once they have been confirmed, may then serve to act as date-indicators elsewhere, at sites with no strati-fication and no opportunity for absolute dating; this applies especially to pottery, so prevalent on African archaeological sites, and which has proved such a useful indicator of date and culture in other parts of the world.

If, then, we can combine the application of all the archaeological dating methods available to us, and if our hopes are fulfilled of the development of additional ones such as the thermoluminescent dating of pottery, there is reason to hope with confidence that we shall soon be able to establish sound chronological frameworks for the various regions of Africa, and thereby obtain a truer perspective on the fascinating history of Africa's past.

CHAPTER FIVE

Traditions and History

Alan Ryder

IN WHATEVER part of the world they may be living, those educated in the European tradition tend to think of history as a body of knowledge based upon documentary evidence: that is to say, upon written records. Much of what has been written to date about African history has relied upon such sources, which are indeed more abundant and fruitful than is often imagined. It remains true, however, that for most of the African continent documentary evidence alone affords only a very imperfect basis for the writing of history. The bulk of the written records available for African history has been produced by non-Africans—many of them having only a brief, imperfect knowledge of the peoples and places they were describing —and the great majority of such papers and writings belong to the past hundred years.

One of the most hopeful means of filling the yawning gaps in our knowledge of Africa's past is contained in the enormous body of material which historians know as oral traditions, or oral evidence. The forms which these oral traditions can assume are extremely varied, so that it is difficult to offer a satisfactory definition embracing them all. For our present purpose it will be sufficient to describe them as the forms in which man relates by word of mouth the past of himself, his ancestors, his rulers or his people. To do so is a natural function of man in any form of organized society; consequently all human groups carry within themselves this basic raw material of their own history.

It is the first of these categories—what a man remembers about his own life—that looms largest in all times and places. It embraces personal experiences and impressions of public events, and most people, as we know, are ready enough to talk about these. Here we have what might be called the first generation of oral tradition: accounts of events that have occurred within the lifetime of those who speak about them. Such memories may be of the utmost value to the historian of Africa, who can use them in place of the diaries, memoirs and biographies available in societies where literary conventions are more firmly established.

In making use of such accounts, we have to take careful note of who is giving them: of his age, position and character; and whether he is speaking privately or before an assembly. Consider, for example, the different values one might attach to the evidence of an aged chief who has served most of his life in the councils of a ruler, and that of a bright young schoolmaster in the same community, if both were asked to tell the history of their town over the past fifty years. The chief might be expected to give an account weighted with understanding and sympathy for the traditional pattern of society, while the schoolmaster might see these years in terms of the welcome arrival of a new order. Their evidence might conflict, even contradict, at many points, but each would be valid and valuable. I shall consider a little later some of the difficulties that arise in collecting and using this kind of evidence. For the moment let me emphasize that these difficulties are not essentially different or greater than those encountered with written documents. Too often it is assumed that anything written must be more reliable than verbal testimony; but every historian knows that a written document needs to be subjected to exactly the same sort of scrutiny as to the circumstances in which it was produced as does a piece of oral evidence. The word of mouth is no more or less subject to distortion, deliberate or accidental, than the written word.

33

The value to the historian of oral tradition of the first generation must, I believe, be fairly obvious. Through it he can obtain access to the events and ideas that have come to pass in the lifetime of living men. In particular they may offer him the non-official or African point of view to set against the official, European attitude that dominates much of the documentary material of African history.

But men do not talk and think only about the events of their own lifetime. They also retell the stories they have heard from their elders about times past, often refashioning or reinterpreting them in order that they may fit more convincingly with the ideas and conditions of the present. Only in very rare circumstances is the account of the past so completely fixed that the teller is forced to subdue entirely his own imaginative and critical faculties. Such conditions usually arise only where a well-established dynasty is able to maintain a court chronicler, whose duty it is to recite an official version of history on state occasions.

An official of this kind was attached to the court of the ruler in the West African kingdom of Benin, and tradition has it that any deviation or lapse of memory on his part was punished by death. Yet even conditions as rigorous as these cannot guarantee that traditions will be handed down unchanged from generation to generation, for they do not prevent an officially inspired change in the approved version of history. Consider, for example, the situation which arises when a junior member of a royal family replaces by force a ruling monarch in a society which places great emphasis upon seniority. The usurper will probably be driven to justify his action by altering the account of the past in such a way as to present himself as the rightful occupant of the throne. In Benin, where struggles for the throne have been common, much ingenuity has been expended in making such alterations of the historical record as are necessary to make 'fact' conform to theory. We have to remember, therefore, that stories about the past, however remote, are essentially stories told in the present, and that they have been subjected to revision by successive generations of story-tellers. Here we have one of the basic differences between written and oral evidence, for while the former acquires a permanent and unalterable form as a material document, the latter is always unfixed and subject to endless modification.

From the historian's point of view the stories which peoples tell about times past may be divided into two general categories. One of these is more consciously historical in purpose and content: that is to say, it represents an effort to relate the story of the past as the people understand it in the light of their beliefs and the information available to them. At the same time, accounts of this kind are usually produced with a utilitarian purpose in view—perhaps to confirm hereditary dignities and possessions, the right to the use of certain lands or waters, or to the services of certain groups within a community. The other category belongs more to the class of imaginative literature, and includes such things as songs in praise of living and dead heroes, incantations used in the worship of gods and ancestors, and the stories employed in divination rites. The historical value and content of such stories, songs and chants is often not very obvious, but they still repay careful study, for the very formality of their structure often preserves odd pieces of information from the variations to which they would be subject in a more obviously historical form of narrative.

Of course oral tradition, like all historical material, has its limitations. In general it would be true to say that it neglects the ordinary and heightens the spectacular, that it tends to interpret events in terms of personal drama. In Benin traditions, for instance, wars are usually represented as the outcome of a personal clash between the ruler and an ambitious subject, and very often a woman features as the cause of the conflict. The traditional historian, Chief Egharevba, gives the following account of a major war

35

fought between Benin and the neighbouring state of Idah in the sixteenth century:

This war was caused by the then Oliha [an important Benin chief] who had a beautiful wife named Imaguero. The Oliha one day said to the king and other people that this wife was the most faithful woman in the whole kingdom. The Oba [king] told him that women were not trustworthy, and, to prove that Imaguero was no exception, the Oba asked one of his porters to go with some coral and agate beads and entice her. On receiving the beads, the woman not only committed adultery, but also obtained leave of her husband to reside in her father's house, where the porter had free and easy access to her. This continued for several weeks. At length the Oba summoned a meeting, and asked the Oliha to repeat what he had said about his wife. [The] Oliha again said without the slightest suspicion that his wife Imaguero was the most faithful woman in the whole kingdom. The porter was presented before the assembly and told to confess what transpired between him and Imaguero. He related how he had been able to win her with only a few beads. Imaguero was then called and she confirmed the statements of the porter. This annoyed the Oliha so much that he instantly ordered her to be strangled. The Oliha did not stop there; in order to bring disaster on the Oba for the trick he had played, he sent his servant to tell the Attah [king] of Idah that the Oba of Benin was preparing to invade his country, and that he should be ready to defend himself. The Attah of Idah mobilized his troops without delay and marched against the Binis [people of Benin].[1]

We may suspect that the king of Idah had more substantial motives for launching this war than those recounted in the story; but this is not to agree with those who maintain that oral tradition oversimplifies its picture of the past. It may, on the contrary, introduce seemingly unnecessary detail in order to produce an explanation of events suited to the particular notions of cause and effect held by the people in question.

Collecting oral tradition for use as historical evidence

[1] J. U. Egharevba, *A Short History of Benin* (3rd ed., 1960), pp. 28–9.

demands above all patience and an understanding of the material—its nature and its limitations. Patience because the collection depends entirely upon the willing coopera- tion of an informant, who must be allowed to tell his story in his own way, even if this appears to introduce much that is irrelevant or misinformed. At all costs the investi- gator must avoid leading questions, but he may be able to guide along certain lines by revealing some of his know- ledge of the period or subject. This may put the informant on his mettle and lead to a useful dialogue. Not only is patience required in the actual recording of information; it is often even more essential in the preliminary stages. An informant is unlikely to pour out his more intimate know- ledge and opinions on first acquaintance with a complete stranger. Therefore the collector of oral tradition must be prepared to spend much time in gaining the friendship and confidence of those among whom he wishes to work before any worthwhile investigation can begin.

There is another general rule for recording oral tradition which also tends to lengthen the proceedings: it is to gather as many versions as possible of a story. When dealing with the history of a state one should seek to record the traditions of the outlying villages as well as those of the capital, where the pressures making for politically inspired alterations may be greater. In any story concerning war or conflict one should of course endeavour to assemble the versions of all the parties involved. Even when the issue appears to be quite straightforward, it often pays to look for variations of the common story, for these may prove to be older versions which will enable one to trace the evolution of the tradition.

Besides patience, the collection and interpretation of oral tradition calls for understanding. The material with which we are dealing seldom, if ever, attempts to give an account of the past in the manner of the modern historian, and if we wish to make use of it for historical purposes we must first try to determine its function at the present time. For example, when enquiring into the origins of a town, we have to realize that the details we are given about such matters as which group arrived first, where the first settlements were made and so forth, are primarily of importance to the people concerned because they determine ownership rights. In other words, they will be more interested in organizing their traditions as a charter for their present advantage than as an objective historical record. Oral traditions are essentially the charters of a non-literate people. Therefore, to accept a story at its face value without first carefully considering its social function is almost certainly to produce a distortion of the historical picture.

While stressing the difficulties that surround the collection and use of oral tradition, I do not wish to give the impression that only professional historians could or should set their hands to the task. On the contrary, the rapid advance of literacy and social transformation throughout Africa calls for a rescue operation on a large scale if a great deal of invaluable information about the past is not to be lost entirely. Already it is becoming difficult to obtain oral tradition uninfluenced by a written source, for there are many local historians who have published versions of traditional history which are eagerly read by their fellow-countrymen. Such histories, which are often entirely praiseworthy in themselves, tend to win a general acceptance and to influence oral tradition. I have known a group of chiefs pause in the middle of a discussion upon some point of tradition to call for the published work of the local historian in order to settle the point at issue. Thus the chances of obtaining genuine oral tradition diminish with the rise of each literate generation, and with the death of those who grew up in a society where that tradition was still a living and potent force.

I hope that I have been able to show that the study of traditions is not an easy or automatic process, but I would urge that it is a worthwhile task to which any dedicated amateur with the interest of his own people at heart ought to turn his attention while the opportunity still exists.

CHAPTER SIX

Documentary Sources for African History

Ivor Wilks

RECENT ADVANCES in African historiography have taken place against a background of what has been aptly termed a data explosion. This has resulted from historians' utilization of material from other disciplines, for example, linguistics and social anthropology; from the development of field techniques for the recording of oral 'texts' of one sort or another; from the growing volume of archaeological work; and not least, from the increasingly systematic study of the available documentary sources—many of which have lain virtually unused until very recent years. In this chapter I shall illustrate something of the variety and nature of this written material, using the West African kingdom of Ashanti as a case study.

Ashanti emerged as a unified kingdom in the last few decades of the seventeenth century. Its first king, the *Asantehene* Osei Tutu, established his capital at Kumasi, some one hundred and twenty miles north of the old Gold Coast on which Dutch, English and Danish trading companies were all firmly established. By the end of the century the first reports on the new power in the interior were appearing in the diaries of the companies' officials. In 1701 the Dutch sent their first ambassador to the court of Osei Tutu, while both Dutch and English began to ply the king with presents, including, for example, a bed with quilted cover and pillow, and a gilded looking glass.

From this time onwards the records of the trading companies contain a constant flow of 'intelligence' upon

Ashanti and its dependencies, for the merchants needed information of this kind if they were to be able to plan their programmes of imports and exports. These reports are now preserved in the metropolitan archives in Europe, in The Hague, London and Copenhagen, surveys of the contents of which are being published by the Athlone Press in the series, *Guides to Materials for West African History*. The Danish and Dutch sources continue to 1850 and 1872 respectively, in which years these two countries abandoned their possessions on the Gold Coast. The English records, however, run unbroken into the period of colonial administration, Ashanti being formally annexed as a Crown Colony in 1902. These sources are extremely rich not only for the study of the relations between Ashanti and the European powers, but also for that of the political, military and constitutional history of Ashanti itself. In the 1740s, for example, the Danes had envoys in Kumasi accredited to the court of the king Opoku Ware. From the reports which they transmitted to the coast of their meeting with the king, we learn something of the extraordinary force of his personality and even curious details of his medical history: he clearly suffered from a disease of the pituitary gland. Moreover, some of these envoys accompanied the large Ashanti army which invaded the northern kingdom of Dagomba in 1744-5: from their accounts we know of the hardship that the troops suffered in their march across the impoverished savannah lands, and of the strange and indecisive military confrontation between the slow-moving Ashanti footmen armed with guns, and the highly mobile Dagomba cavalry equipped only with swords, lances and bows. In 1817, to take another example, T. E. Bowdich spent about four months in Kumasi as agent of the British African Company, negotiating a treaty of trade and friendship with the king. Bowdich's despatches, and the book which he published in 1819, *Mission from Cape Coast Castle to Ashantee*, give an extraordinary wealth of detail about the capital at that time, including information about court ritual, military organization, urban architecture and the prices of commodities in the market.

Ashanti however maintained commercial links not only with the European companies on the Gold Coast to its south, but also with the great Muslim-dominated entre-pôts on and beyond the Niger to its north. Indeed, in the first half of the eighteenth century Ashanti had thrust its frontiers northwards to incorporate as provinces countries like Gonja, Dagomba and Gyaman in which there were Muslim trading communities having links with the greater centres further north. In the Arabic writings of the Muslim scholars of these communities one thus finds further references to Ashanti affairs. The mid-eighteenth-century *Kitab Ghunja* (see page 13) contains, for example, dated notices of the Ashanti expansion into this northern hinterland; of particular interest, since it illustrates the early Muslim reaction to the Ashanti overlordship, is the obituary of the king Opoku Ware, who died in 1750:

. . . may God curse him and put his soul into hell. It was he who harmed the people of Gonja, oppressing them and robbing them of their property at his will. He reigned violently as a tyrant, enjoying his authority. Peoples of the horizons feared him much. He had a long reign of almost forty years. He was succeeded by his maternal aunt's son Kusi.

Relations between the Ashanti kings and the Muslims improved subsequently, and by the beginning of the nineteenth century the *Asantehene* and the rulers of the northern provinces conducted correspondence with each other through their *imams* and other Muslim functionaries. Strangely enough, a number of such letters were found recently in the Royal Library in Copenhagen. One of them, dated about 1808, is of particular interest in that it reports a decision of the Ashanti king and council to set free and repatriate all enslaved Muslims in Ashanti. By this time the Ashanti government was attempting to create in Kumasi an Arabic chancery, and Muslims were employed to keep records of court proceedings, administrative decisions and the like. It is probable that most of this material was destroyed when the British briefly occupied Kumasi in 1874 and burned the town. Apart from the material in Copenhagen, one item that has survived is an Arabic transcript of the negotiations between Ashanti and British missions which met at the Pra River in 1881. This report, interestingly enough, was prepared for the British by their government Arabist in Sierra Leone, for onward despatch to the *Asantehene*. In this century English has replaced Arabic as the language of the Ashanti administration; the voluminous records of the proceedings of the State Council, for example, are all in this language. They are of particular interest to the historian, since so much of the evidence presented before the Council consisted of oral 'texts' of the kind mentioned in Chapters Two and Five; these records, in other words, contain the earliest recensions of much material previously transmitted verbally.

Sources in English, Dutch, Danish and Arabic have been mentioned. In addition reference must be made to the occasional writings of Portuguese, German and French traders and travellers; to a few recent works in Twi, the language of the Ashanti; and to items in Hausa concerned particularly with the growth of the Muslim trading community in Kumasi in this century. It will be apparent that linguistic versatility is not least among the accomplishments required of the historian of Ashanti. Ashanti was of course an extremely powerful kingdom in the eighteenth and nineteenth centuries, and was economically well-endowed. The extraordinary richness of the documentary sources clearly reflects these facts. It is true in general, however, that for many parts of Africa the quest for documentary materials is bringing to light an unexpectedly rich range of sources for the reconstruction of the continent's past.

There are works of African history the authors of which

have relied almost entirely upon documentary sources. Claridge's *History of the Gold Coast and Ashanti,* published in 1915, is based for example almost exclusively upon English official materials, and it is significant that of its thirteen hundred pages over three-quarters are devoted to the period 1800–1900. It is now becoming generally recognized, however, that the satisfactory reconstruction of the African past must depend upon a synthesis of all available data, and in particular that an adequate interpretation of the documentary sources is often possible only when these can be correlated with field material; that is, with orally transmitted narratives. One case will exemplify this general point. In 1707 a party of Ashanti traders sent by the king arrived at the Dutch trading post of Axim on the western Gold Coast. They wished to make considerable purchases of guns and gunpowder. As a matter of course the Dutch officials asked the reasons for these purchases, and were told that the *Asantehene* intended to despatch a punitive expedition against a certain Ntow Kuroko who had rebelled against him. This was duly recorded by the Dutch, and their reports may still be consulted in the Dutch archives. But this is all we learn from them; we know neither who Ntow Kuroko was, nor the reason for his rebellion. To both of these questions, however, Ashanti oral sources provide answers. The traditionalists at the Ashanti court speak of Ntow Kuroko as chief of a once important town south of Kumasi, called Boaman, and say that he became alienated from the king when a subject of Boaman, Adu Yeboa, was appointed over his head to high office within the king's army. In such a case it is the documentary sources which establish the historicity of the events and locate them in time, but it is the oral ones which enable the actors to be identified, and the events to be placed in the wider context of Ashanti history.

Documents may of course fail to refer to important events simply because these do not come to the attention of a *rapporteur*. In oral narratives, however, all reference to events may be suppressed because these cease to be of relevance to (or indeed become positively disruptive of) the socio-political life of the community. An interesting case of the latter phenomenon is that of the *Bandahene*'s skull. When Bowdich was in Kumasi in 1817 he was told of an expedition which an earlier Ashanti king had conducted against the north-western province of Banda, in the course of which the ruler of the area, the *Bandahene*, had been slain and his skull taken to Kumasi to be placed upon one of the great drums there. Three years later Dupuis visited Kumasi (see Chapter Two), and was assured by Ashanti and Muslims alike that there had been no such war against Banda and that the information about a skull was quite wrong. What seems to have happened was that between the visits to Kumasi of Bowdich and Dupuis, the Ashanti had fought a campaign against Gyaman, and in the course of this the then *Bandahene* had not only served loyally on the Ashanti side but had indeed virtually saved the day for the Ashanti forces. In such circumstances it will be apparent that all references to the earlier hostilities between Ashanti and Banda had become dysfunctional: the Banda had now proven their loyalty, the *Bandahene*'s skull was removed from the state drum, and all talk of the circumstances of his death suppressed as harmful gossip.

A somewhat similar case may be instanced from the Gonja state in northern Ghana. According to the traditionalists, the creation of the kingdom was the work of one Jakpa, who is said to have migrated thence from 'Mande', i.e. Mali, at the head of a band of horsemen. The mid-eighteenth-century *Kitab Ghunja* does indeed refer to Jakpa, and assigns his reign to the years 1622/3–1666/7. According to this work, however, Jakpa was the fifth ruler of Gonja, and it was the first, Nabaga, who had founded the kingdom and who (by implication) had arrived from Mali. The oral sources contain the clue as to why the earlier kings have been forgotten by the traditionalists. They tell how, during the reign of Jakpa, Gonja was organized into

44

divisions and each placed under a 'son' of Jakpa. Thus, from the point of view of the Gonja traditionalists, who are concerned first and foremost with constitutional matters, all that occurred before the time of Jakpa is irrelevant, since problems of succession to the divisional chiefships are resolved by reference to the administrative structure created by Jakpa and his 'sons'. Logically, then, the orally transmitted accounts regard Gonja history as commencing with Jakpa, and it is only from the early literary sources that we learn anything of the pre-Jakpa period.

Orally transmitted material, then, is subject to revisionary processes which necessitate great care in its utilization for purposes of historical reconstruction. Although the considerable volume of documentary material available to the historian of Africa has been emphasized in this chapter, it remains the case that this material is frequently of a fragmentary kind, referring to this or that event but often in insufficient detail to permit a definitive reconstruction of the major movements of the period. The historian is in a particularly favourable position when he is able to combine both documentary and oral sources, and many of the more exciting developments in the discipline in recent years have resulted from just this possibility. The continuing development of African historical studies must depend both upon the extensive and scientific recording of oral material—a matter still in its infancy—and upon the relentless search for documentary materials in the archives and public and private libraries not only of Africa itself, but of Europe, America and Asia. Early nineteenth-century correspondence between the Ashanti king and the rulers of his northern provinces could turn up in Copenhagen; the Prime Minister's Archives in Istanbul contain letters from the Sultan to the ruler of Bornu in West Africa dating from the sixteenth century; an emancipated slave could write down in Arabic, in Jamaica in 1834, an account of his early life in Timbuctu and Jenne and of his education in

Buna.[1] The documentary field offers exciting prospects for the historian, and the locating, translating, editing and publishing of such material will engage the attention of scholars for many years.

[1] For these last two examples see the article by B. G. Martin, 'Kanem, Bornu, and the Fazzan', *Journal of African History*, Vol. X, No. 1 (1969), and the story of Abu Bakr al-Siddiq as presented by Ivor Wilks in Philip D. Curtin, *Africa Remembered* (1967).

CHAPTER SEVEN

Arabic Sources for African History

John Hunwick

ON A HOT Saturday morning in May 1967, I made my way
on foot through the narrow crowded lanes of the old city
of Fez to the ancient library of the Qarawiyyin mosque at
Suq al-Saffarin—the brass workers' market. The object of
my visit, which had brought me the previous day from
Rabat, some one hundred and twenty miles away, was to
see manuscript volumes of an Arabic dictionary, the
Muhkam of Ibn Sida, which in its entirety is almost the
size of the *Encyclopedia Britannica*. What, one may ask,
has this to do with African history? The answer will perhaps show to what lengths the modern historian of Africa
may sometimes have to go in his efforts to build up a
detailed picture of life in Africa during a period which one
eminent British historian could recently still refer to as
'the age of darkness'.[1] I discovered, on a closer examination,
that these two volumes of the dictionary had been copied
in Timbuctu during the years 1574 and 1575; they had
evidently been brought back to Fez following the Moroccan
conquest of the Niger bend in 1591. On the last pages were
details of the names of the copyists and their ancestors, the
person who employed them, and the fees paid both for
copying and for correcting the copy. The discovery that this
enormous work of erudition had been studied in sixteenth-
century Timbuctu was in itself a strong argument to fortify
that city's claim to have been a major intellectual centre
in Africa; for the historian who is interested in more than

[1] See page 7.

47

just 'battles and dates', the other details were equally precious.

The past decade has witnessed a revolution in our knowledge of the African past, partly through the exploitation of European sources, and partly through archaeological discoveries and the use of oral tradition. But at the same time a great deal of work has been quietly going on in collecting and analysing materials in Arabic, and the coming decade seems likely to produce another revolution in our knowledge based on these materials.

A word first about the scope of these materials. Firstly, Arabic materials are only available for the Muslim or predominantly Muslim areas of Africa—in general north of the tenth degree of latitude, except in East Africa, where Islamic influence stretches down the coast to the borders of Mozambique. In point of time they only cover the period of Muslim influence; that is, in North Africa from the mid-seventh century, and in East and West Africa fragmentarily from about the tenth century, with local chronicles first appearing in West Africa not until the early sixteenth century. Not surprisingly for North Africa, Arabic materials form the main source for the historian throughout this period until the colonial era, though Spanish, Portuguese and Ottoman Turkish sources are important at certain periods. In East Africa, while Arabic and Swahili documents are important for pre-nineteenth-century history, there are other sources, notably Portuguese ones, to supplement them.

It is for the savannah lands of West Africa from Lake Chad to the Atlantic that the Arabic materials are so vital. For the period up to the nineteenth century virtually no other original written materials exist, apart from Leo Africanus's brief accounts (originally written in Arabic anyhow), and the odd snippets of information picked up by European explorers and merchants on the coast at third and fourth hand about distant areas they had never seen. It is, therefore, on this area, generally known as the western Sudan, that I shall concentrate most of my remarks.

What kinds of Arabic material have scholars been looking for and working on over the past few years? Firstly,
there are the accounts of the western Sudan by outside
authors, most of whom never set foot in the area. However,
such men as the eleventh-century Spanish geographer
al-Bakri, the mid-fourteenth-century Egyptian scholar
al-'Umari and the famous historian Ibn Khaldun, writing
in the latter part of the same century, made use of information obtained from African diplomats and scholars whom
they met in North Africa and Egypt. The most valuable of
all these external sources, however, is the first-hand account
given by the fourteenth-century Moroccan globe-trotter,
Ibn Battuta, who had already visited Ceylon and China
and had travelled down the East African coast as far as
Kilwa in 1329. This intrepid traveller crossed the Mauri-
tanian deserts in 1352 and reached the capital of the old
kingdom of Mali, well to the south of modern Bamako,
returning to North Africa by way of Timbuctu, Gao and
the central Sahara. His descriptions, along with those of
al-'Umari, give us a vivid and detailed picture of life in the
Mali empire at the height of its power.

The earliest local historical writing we know of so far
dates only from the early sixteenth century, though it
relates, in part, the events of earlier periods. From the
hands of three generations of scholars of the Ka'ti family
of Jenne, we have a compendious history of the Songhai
down to the Moroccan conquest of 1591. A little later, from
the Timbuctu historian al-Sa'di, we have the even more
extensive *Ta'rikh al-Sudan*, which partly covers the same
period, but also carries the narrative down to 1655. Finally,
from an anonymous author there is a detailed history of the
rule of the Moroccan pashas of Timbuctu from 1591 to
1751.

From Timbuctu the tradition of chronicle- or *ta'rikh*-
writing spread to other areas. The Ivory Coast and Ghana
have a tradition of local village and clan chronicles going
back to the mid-eighteenth century, though its roots clearly

antedate this and probably derive ultimately from Timbuctu. Nigeria, too, has proved a fertile ground for local Arabic chroniclers. Earliest of these is Ibn Fartuwa, who has left us a fascinating account of the life and times of *Mai* Idris of Bornu in the late sixteenth century. By the early nineteenth century, during the *jihad* period, we have an abundance of both general and local chronicles, as well as biographies of some of the rulers. Biography has always been a popular form of Muslim writing. There are in existence a number of collections of brief lives of the scholars and saints of Timbuctu and southern Mauritania, giving us precious details of the religious and intellectual life of the area from the fifteenth to the nineteenth centuries.

Correspondence, both local and international, is one of our most important historical sources, for letters are completely raw material—history, as it were, speaking for itself. For the pre-nineteenth-century period only isolated examples have so far come to light—among them a letter from Bornu to Egypt dated 1391; a letter written in 1578 by the Ottoman sultan in Istanbul to the *Mai* Idris of Bornu, recently discovered in the Turkish archives; and letters from the Sultan of Morocco to the *Askia* of Songhai and the *Kanta* of Kebbi—all dating from the 1590s—which I was able to see in Morocco recently.

From the nineteenth century, correspondence is to be found in great abundance, particularly in Nigeria, where the administration of the large empire established by Usuman dan Fodio depended for its good government on close liaison between the headquarters in Sokoto and the various emirates. Correspondence from Seku Ahmadu's empire of Masina in what is now Mali has also come to light.

Finally there is a category which I simply call odds and ends, and this is an almost literal description. I mean principally such things as notes by copyists at the ends of books—no matter what the subject of the book is—such as the one mentioned at the beginning of this chapter. These can be very valuable in cross-checking chronologies. Such a note at the end of a clan-history recently discovered in Northern Nigeria states that the work was copied in 1651, 'at the beginning of the reign of the Sultan of Kano, Muhammad Kukuna'; a letter on Islamic government sent by the Algerian scholar al-Maghili to Sultan Ibrahim of Katsina is dated 1492, and is quoted in a work of the nine-teenth-century reformer Dan Fodio; a copy of a famous Muslim law book I saw in Rabat was made for *Askia* Muhammad Bani of Gao and dated 1587. All these scraps of information from unlikely sources help us broadly to confirm chronologies that have until now been considered very tentative.

These, then, are the main categories of Arabic material, but before evaluating them, I would like to make a brief mention of another type of material that is now coming to light in increasing quantity. I refer to documents in African languages—Hausa, Fulfulde, Mande, Kanuri and Swahili, to name but a few—written in Arabic characters. They are mostly, but not wholly, concerned with religious matters, and are often in verse, but even so can be of great value for building up a more coherent picture of the religious and social life of African people. Needless to say, the linguists are already finding them useful for the study of the historical development of African languages.

Like any category of historical material, the Arabic sources should not be relied on in isolation, without checks and balances to correct their perspectives. We should not forget that they were the product of men who viewed the world in terms of a particular ideology. Events are seen against a background of Islam as the unique, divinely inspired system of government and way of life. References to non-Muslim peoples are scarce, and such people and their governments are generally pictured as anarchic bar-barians or 'enemies of God'. The writers, too, were all from a particular stratum of society, either court chroniclers and scribes, or the scholarly upper class of *imams* and jurists; not surprisingly their works reflect the aspirations of this class. We must also take care not to be over-enthusiastic simply because these are *written* sources. European historians have tended to view the written word as almost sacred, but much of what has been written, in the chronicles in particular, is based on earlier oral tradition, and was only written down decades and sometimes centuries after the event. Each written source must be critically evaluated before reliance is put on it.

Against these limitations we should, however, set the following positive criteria. Firstly, the Arabic materials provide a solid base for the study of many areas, and often provide a counterbalance to the accounts given by oral tradition and European sources. Secondly, the less directly historical works are important for giving us some insight into social and religious values, into political and administrative theory, and both popular and higher education in pre-colonial days. Last, but not least, for the nineteenth and early twentieth centuries, they present the 'other side of the story' which has been all too little heard amid the overwhelming clamour of European colonial views. The Arabic documents relating to such anti-colonial resistance movements as those of Samori in the Ivory Coast, Babatu in Northern Ghana and the Sokoto caliphate in Northern Nigeria do, in spite of their limitations, represent authentic African voices speaking about their own history and traditions. They shed light on many a dark corner only previously illuminated by an equally committed set of opposing views—those of the Christian missionary, European trader and colonial administrator. For this, above all, we must be grateful.

CHAPTER EIGHT

Historians and West Africa

David Birmingham

THE MODERN tradition of West African historical writing goes back twenty years to the founding of the great universities of Legon and Ibadan in the last years of colonial rule. One of the first demands of the rising generation of African undergraduates was that they should study history in depth in the new universities. An interest in history was deeply rooted in African tradition and was an important and living part of daily culture. What was new twenty years ago was the broadened scope and perspective with which history was viewed by teachers and students in the emerging universities. History was no longer perceived as the history of immediate forbears and of neighbouring villages, clans and states. History was now interpreted to cover the broad sweep of human endeavour and achievement in West Africa and in the world beyond. This new tradition of historical scholarship was even broader than the medieval tradition of Islamic scholarship which for the past millennium had widened the horizons of some West African scholars.

In attempting to portray the West African past, historians sought advice from other specialists. Archaeologists studied the material remains of man's activity in order to categorize the major stages of West African historical development. Over a period of several hundred thousand years the early occupants of West Africa gradually improved their range of skills, techniques and tools used for hunting and gathering. Their first great economic breakthrough may have come with the development of fishing, soon to be followed by farming and other regular forms of food production. During the last centuries before Christ some West Africans began to improve their tools and weapons still further with the adoption of metal-working techniques. As yet more is known about the tools of these early West Africans than about the people themselves, but a recent archaeological find in Nigeria suggests that by ten thousand years ago their features were similar to those of present-day inhabitants.[1]

In studying the early pre-history of West Africa before the familiar peoples and states had begun to take shape, the historian may also look to the linguist for help. A striking feature of the languages of West Africa is their sharp differentiation from each other. Whereas many of the languages of northern Africa form part of the Erythraic or Afro-Asiatic 'family', and many of the languages of Central and Southern Africa are related within the Bantu group, West Africa forms part of a linguistic 'fragmentation belt' stretching from Senegal to Ethiopia, in which the historical classification of languages, in spite of Greenberg's work, is still very uncertain. When the relationships (and non-relationships) of these languages have been more adequately established, patterns of association may provide information about historical links between peoples at an earlier date than can be gained from oral traditions. In the meantime the pattern of fragmentation must be interpreted to mean that during the Iron Age, and probably before, a great variety of West African groups have developed cultural traditions of their own, in comparative isolation and without being affected by foreign influences sufficiently strong or widespread to interrupt the local pattern of language development.[2]

[1] See Oliver Davies, *West Africa before the Europeans* (1967) and Raymond Mauny, *Tableau Géographique de l'Ouest Africain au Moyen Age* (Dakar, 1961); Brian Fagan, 'Carbon Dates for sub-Saharan Africa', *Journal of African History*, Vol. X No. 1 (1969), p. 151.

[2] For examples of historical writing in which linguistic evidence has been used, see *Ghana Notes and Queries*, 1966, and David Dalby (ed.),

As historians move towards the study of the more recent past, they have naturally been much interested in the formation of states, kingdoms and empires. In this field, concerned mainly with the last five hundred years except for a few studies of the empires of the western and central Sudan, their source material has been both more wide-spread and more conventional. Historians have in particular greatly benefited from the writings of anthropologists and Islamists of the colonial period, many of them adminis-trators who took an intelligent interest in the peoples whom they had been appointed to rule. It is on the pioneer studies of men such as Delafosse, Rattray, Palmer and Urvoy that modern scholars have built their new school of history; they have added new questions, new hypotheses and new problems, and in their endeavour to solve them they have quarried deeper into the two main categories of historical data available for the pre-colonial period.[3]

The first category of data is, of course, oral tradition. This is valuable as a record not only of important state governments, but also of individual families, political offices, hereditary ceremonial positions, and a wide variety of clans, villages and shrines. In recent years, for instance, an impressive project has been under way to collect several hundred 'stool histories' in Ashanti in Ghana. From this mass of data, scholars are now studying the nature of Ashanti government, the relations between the various states of the union, the manner in which offices were created and office-holders preferred, and the process of Ashanti expansion among the satellite Akan states.

The second major category of historical data which has been used with increasing intensity is the reports of foreign travellers in West Africa. In the north, and in some forest

---

Language and History in Africa (Frank Cass, forthcoming). The term 'linguistic fragmentation belt' is Dalby's.

[3] Maurice Delafosse, *Haut–Sénégal–Niger* (Paris, 1912); R. S. Rattray, *Ashanti Law and Constitution* (Oxford, 1929); H. R. Palmer, *Sudanese Memoirs* (Lagos, 1928); Yves Urvoy, *Histoire du Bornu* (Paris, 1949).

regions as well, Arabic-speaking travellers have given accounts of the markets, cities and kingdoms which they visited. Some of these literate travellers of the Islamic world settled as teachers and chancellors, and established literary records even in some non-Muslim states. Much useful work remains to be done in unearthing historical manuscripts in Arabic script. In the southern part of West Africa, the foreign records are mainly European accounts. A dramatic example of their potential has been shown by a recent reconstruction of the history of Mande influence in Upper Guinea based predominantly on sixteenth-century Portuguese materials.[4] The Portuguese records have also done much to amplify the traditional interpretations of Benin history, and they may one day be used to cast light on the early kingdoms and mining communities of the Gold Coast. Recent historical work has also uncovered a wealth of valuable information in the archives of Denmark and Holland, containing not only descriptions of West African states, but in one case local manuscripts recorded in Arabic script.[5] Very good use can also be made of the pre-colonial accounts of British and French visitors to West Africa, as shown in an exciting recent study of the kingdom of Dahomey, in which the pioneer eighteenth-century works of Norris and Dalzel have been reassessed in the light of unpublished European records.[6] It is to be hoped that similar studies will follow dealing with Benin, Akim, Tekrur and the many other important West African kingdoms whose history has not yet been adequately investigated.

Historians of the pre-colonial period have usually been more successful in dealing with political history than in treating economic history. The recurrent theme of West

[4] Walter Rodney, 'A History of the Upper Guinea Coast 1545–1800'. Unpublished Ph.D. thesis (London, 1966).

[5] Nehemia Levtzion, *Muslims and Chiefs in West Africa* (1968); K. Y. Daaku, *Trade and Politics on the Gold Coast* (Oxford, 1969) makes good use of Dutch material.

[6] I. A. Akinjogbin, *Dahomey and its Neighbours* (Cambridge, 1967).

African history has been 'trade and politics', but trade has often come off second best. One of the difficulties has been obtaining information about local enterprises, industries, crafts, markets, methods of transport, labour recruitment and commodity supplies. Although oral tradition, when collected from the different interest-groups and when critically examined, will often give useful political, social and military information, it rarely gives details of everyday commercial and industrial pursuits, and often does not inform the historian even about external trade. The Atlantic slave trade itself, probably the most widespread commercial influence which foreigners brought to West Africa, is but scantily understood in terms of the effects which it had on West African society and economic development. The history of iron working and trading, salt distribution, ivory hunting, copper marketing, weaving, potting, and the many other specialist crafts which lay at the base of the West African economy, still awaits extensive investigation in most parts of the region.[7]

The last twenty years have seen much work on the prehistorical and pre-colonial periods of history, but it is in the modern period that the most radical reassessments are likely to be made. The writing of colonial history will pass from the colonial ex-rulers to the colonial ex-subjects. The reassessment will be a complex, fluctuating and much disputed one. It is still too early to judge whether in retrospect the colonial period will appear as an earthshaking era of irreversible change, or merely as a half-century of evolution much like any other. It can be argued either that the colonial period constituted an era of rapid modernization, or that it was a period of stagnation in which the introduction of a few railways and coin currencies failed to compensate for the degree to which Africa was falling behind in

[7] For examples of the type of problem which might be worth further study see Richard Gray and David Birmingham (eds.), *Pre-Colonial African Trade* (1969). See also the numerous articles on Western Nigerian economic history by Dr A. G. Hopkins.

the development of the world. The colonizers can be seen as the purveyors of education and technology or as the exploiters of unpaid-for raw materials, or simply as participants in a gigantic game of diplomatic chess.

So far attempts to interpret the colonial period have been undertaken more by Europeans and Americans than by Africans themselves. Perhaps to many Africans the subject has been too much obscured by the flamboyant, though not necessarily inaccurate, interpretations of politicians, to be impartially analysed without emotional involvement. West African historians have thus far tended to concentrate on fringe subjects of the colonial period. One which has commanded a surprising degree of interest is the impact of Christianity on Africa. Detailed studies have been made of numerous missions, churches and independent religious groups.[8] It may be that this emphasis will prove fruitful, and that in the long term the effects of Christian missions will appear more lasting—whether in a positive or a negative sense—than the effects of colonial rule.

In modern times, the writing of history in West Africa, which began with the demands of students, has largely remained in the universities, now over a dozen in number. Other historians have published specialist accounts of their own cities or secondary accounts designed for school children,[9] but the majority of new, analytical history is still carried out in the universities by teachers and graduate students. The University of Ibadan, in particular, built a strong graduate school of history with both an older and a younger generation of teachers trained in the modern methods of African historiography. Predominantly undergraduate schools also developed at other English-speaking universities—Legon, Fourah Bay, Ife, Nsukka, Zaria—so

[8] For instance J. F. A. Ajaye, *Christian Missions in Nigeria* (1965); F. L. Bartels, *The Roots of Ghana Methodism* (Cambridge, 1965).

[9] E. J. Alagoa, *The Small Brave City State* (Madison, U.S.A., 1964); F. K. Buah, *A New History for West African Schools and Colleges* (?1964) are examples of recent history written outside the universities.

that many secondary school teachers in English-speaking West Africa have taken degrees in the history of Africa.

In French-speaking Africa the tradition has been a little different. As in France, research and teaching tend to be two separate academic compartments. The former was well catered for in West Africa, and local outposts of the Institut Français d'Afrique Noire fostered research into historical problems of Cameroun, Dahomey, Senegal and Mali. Teaching came only later and is but slowly beginning to train African undergraduates, many of whom were brought up in the classical French tradition of 'nos ancêtres, les Gaulois . . .'.

The last twenty years has seen the re-creating of a tradition according to which Africa is recognized as having a history, just like every other continent, albeit one which requires new techniques unfamiliar to scholars trained on European source material. In the process a great deal has been learnt about the historical role of archaeology, which has dramatically moved from simply classifying artefacts to reconstructing the political, social and economic activities of their users. New ways of interpreting, cross-checking and supporting oral traditions have been devised, so that oral evidence is no longer taken at its face value without critical interpretation—any more than the documents of a European chancery are. Finally the historian must constantly return to the old and well-known sources to seek the light they may cast on the changing questions and hypotheses which he is forever formulating.

The next twenty years should see even more dramatic progress in the field of West African history. The present situation has been reached by a handful of pioneers who have inspired a few hundred followers. The process of growth must continue, and the next two decades should reflect increasingly detailed field work on specific regions and problems. Moreover, as the colonial period recedes, its image will become sharper, and its place in the historical panorama will be more clearly perceived.

CHAPTER NINE

Historians and North Africa

Anthony Atmore

As it is impossible in a chapter of this length to consider in any detail the great range of historical work now in progress in and about North Africa, I shall confine myself to a discussion of some of the major themes which interest both historians of this region and myself, an external observer of their activities. Most of what I have to say will be about North-West Africa, known to the Arabs as the Maghrib. This is a part of the world rich in layer upon layer of the history of civilized and of not so civilized communities, which has had its own universities for hundreds of years, and its own traditions of writing about history. Ibn Khaldun, one of the great historians of all time, was born in Tunis in the fourteenth century, and spent most of his life in North Africa or Muslim Spain. His present-day successors, teachers both in the old Muslim universities such as Fez, and in the modern ones at Rabat, Algiers, Tunis and Benghazi, are likewise pursuing their enquiries into their countries' past. In Morocco, the rector of the Mohammad V University at Rabat, Mohammad al-Fasi, has published several works on the Alawid dynasty of sultans. There is an important research institute at this university, the Centre Universitaire de la Recherche Scientifique. At Tetwan is the Instituto Muley el-Hassan, founded by the Spaniards, which publishes the historical journal *Hesperis-Tamuda*. As well as these North Africans, many French and Spanish scholars have become specialists in Maghribi history; this is not surprising, since France and Spain ruled the Maghrib during the colonial period. One of the great authorities on the history of the Maghrib is Professor Roger le Tourneau of the University of Aix and Marseilles; le Tourneau is an economic historian and sociologist, and has written on the urban proletariat and on the modern history of North Africa. His *magnum opus* is a sociological study of the city of Fez before the French Protectorate.[1] At Aix-en-Provence is the Centre pour l'Étude de l'Afrique Méditerranéenne. Its very name, to a lecturer in African history like myself, is indicative of certain attitudes towards North Africa.

I have specialized in studying parts of the continent far removed from the North, and have to admit to being an outsider in the history of the Maghrib. Until recently there has been, as far as the writing of history is concerned, an almost unbridged gulf between North Africa and the rest of the continent. Historians either studied Africa south of the Sahara, or Africa north of the great desert. The latter was considered to be part of the Muslim Middle Eastern world, or part of the Mediterranean world; but not part of Africa historically speaking. These ways of looking at North Africa are perfectly valid. The Sahara *is* a formidable barrier, coming between the Mediterranean coast lands and the rest of Africa. But this is not the whole story. The great desert has been crossed and re-crossed for thousands of years. North Africa is not *merely* a geographical part of Africa; it is also a part of the history of Africa.

An example of the many medieval literary bridges across the Sahara was the record of the fourteenth-century Maghribi traveller, Ibn Battuta. Nineteenth-century European travellers followed in the footsteps of their Muslim predecessors, and have left invaluable accounts of their journeys. But it was not until E. W. Bovill published *The Caravans of the Old Sahara* in 1933 that English readers were presented with a work that integrated the history of

---

[1] le Tourneau, Roger, *Fès avant le protectorate: Étude économique et sociale d'une ville de l'occident musulman* (Casablanca, 1949).

the Maghrib, the Sahara and the Sudanic region of West Africa.[2] It is significant that one of the most important ventures in this field is the work of a Ghanaian professor of history, Adu Boahen, entitled *Britain, the Sahara and the Western Sudan 1788–1861*, and published in 1964.

The treatment of the Sahara as a kind of ocean is one of the great North African historical themes. Across it flowed peoples—many alas as slaves—who modified the existing populations to the north and to the south; West Africa was the principal supplier of gold to Europe and the Mediterranean lands during the Middle Ages, and the precious dust was carried in little bags across the desert; goods of great value and craftsmanship passed between black men and brown-skinned Arabs and Berbers; languages were carried across the burning sands, as were ideas and religious faiths. These are the bonds which unified the North and the rest of Africa, which originated before Islam, and spread wider than the confines of this religion.

There are many similarities, and many parallels, between the history of North and of sub-Saharan Africa. What has emerged over the last decade as a topic of major interest to historians of sub-Saharan Africa is the reactions of African peoples to the penetration of Europeans and to the imposition of colonial rule. The roots of modern African nationalism, the seeds of the independence movement, can be traced to the various manifestations of resistance by Africans. What is so fascinating to someone like myself who has studied these reactions, is that the Maghrib has experienced the same process for centuries. Today the Maghrib is predominantly Arabic in speech and Muslim in culture; some of the present population are descendants of Arab nomadic groups, the Bedouin, who migrated across North Africa from Arabia from the eleventh century onwards—not, it should be noted, from the time of the initial conquests of the Maghrib by Arab

[2] The book was rewritten in 1958 as *The Golden Trade of the Moors*, and thoroughly revised in 1968 by Robin Hallett.

adventurers in the seventh and eighth centuries. Berber-speakers are now largely confined to inaccessible mountain regions. But this has not always been so. The process by which the Berbers, with their own language, their own institutions, their own culture, have been transformed into Arabic-speaking Muslims, has been exceedingly complex. One reason for this was the loose nature of Berber political institutions. Berber society was made up of small groups, villages in the mountain valleys, or nomadic bands in the desert, which were basically democratic and autonomous. A certain number of these little republics formed a some-what amorphous unit that can be called a tribe; and a number of tribes were tenuously linked to form what French sociologists call Confederations. Members of the great Berber Confederations, such as Sanhaja and Zenata, were scattered throughout the Maghrib. The tribal and con-federate institutions only functioned in times of dire crisis, when, faced with alien penetration, the villager so valued his independence that he was prepared to sink his indi-viduality and join his fellows in a wider military and political grouping. But there was never any united resist-ance. The Confederations were bitterly hostile to one another; if one were openly defying foreign intrusions, at least one other would be siding with the enemy.

This great theme of intense sectional loyalties resulting in overall disunity runs right through Maghribi history. When the Berbers did succumb to the influences of Islam, they characteristically adapted unorthodox forms of the new religion. The tremendous series of rebellions during the first few centuries of Arab penetration were inspired by fanatical Muslim sects, as were the two great medieval empires, the Almoravid and the Almohad. Each was pri-marily the creation of one Confederation, the Almoravid empire of the Sanhaja and the Almohad of the Zenata, and not of the Berber people as a whole. The Almohad empire of the twelfth century was the last flowering of Berber political power. Thereafter the migrations of the

Bedouin disrupted Berber society still further. Resistance to authority, be it in the form of native Arab/Berber dynasties or the Ottoman Turks, was by little independent theocracies, set up by the adherents of religious leaders. In the nineteenth and twentieth centuries the French and Spaniards met with fierce resistance which was, however, weakened by this almost anarchical state of disunity. What is of great interest to many Maghribi and French historians is how out of these disparate groups a powerful nationalist movement evolved. One of the answers to this question must be found in the rapid urbanization which was a feature of the Maghrib in colonial times.

It is not surprising that much of the historical work on the Maghrib should be markedly sociological in content. The changes brought about by the impact of European rule and technology have been as disturbing as any in other parts of Africa or Asia. Casablanca is a concrete example of such changes. It was a fishing village until the early 1900s, when the French started to construct a modern harbour and to build a railway to the phosphate mines of the interior. In the space of sixty years it has grown into a huge city, as large as any in North Africa except Cairo. Casablanca has its port, its industrial areas, its fine suburbs and its periphery of shanty towns, in which tens of thousands of poor people live in degrading slums. These people have flocked to Casablanca, as they have been lured to all the great North African cities, from all over the country —from the plains, from the mountain valleys and from the desert. They have been thrown violently together, living close-packed in strange surroundings, working at unfamiliar jobs. A whole range of questions has to be asked about them—how they adapted to their new situations, whether they kept ties with their home districts, what effect schooling had on them, what kind of associations, political and others, they formed, how they gave vent to their discontent. Most of such questions can be answered by a sociologist, and many workers both in the Maghrib and in France have embarked upon studies of urbanization, of trade unions, of changes in the pattern of family life as well as of the growth of political parties. Nationalism, which in Morocco and Tunisia had to overcome rather half-hearted French opposition to achieve independence, but which in Algeria had to fight many grim years to do so, is to the historian but the latest manifestation of a very ancient, very deep-seated determination on the part of the people of the Maghrib to resist alien influences and the rule of foreigners.

Maghribi historians are concerned to explain why their peoples succumbed to foreign rule, and at the same time are concerned to push the roots of nationalism as far down into the earth of history as they can; thus the Almoravids and the Almohads have been seen as early examples of Maghribi 'nationalism'. French historians are, to some extent, concerned to justify what was done in the name of France in North Africa. Motives such as these, which can exist quite legitimately alongside a genuine search for historical 'truth', are themselves part and parcel of the historical process, and can be paralleled elsewhere in Africa. To me, even a cursory acquaintance with North African history is of great relevance to the understanding of the history of the continent as a whole.

CHAPTER TEN

Historians and East Africa

Bethwell A. Ogot

EAST AFRICAN history, like much of African history, was until after the Second World War mainly the concern of amateurs. As foreign observers of the East African scene, and with their diverse backgrounds—proconsular or administrative, missionary or settler—they not only inaugurated the study of the region's history; they also created 'pioneer traditions' which still influence enormously the study of East African history.

Among the works of proconsuls and administrators mention might be made of F. J. D. Lugard's polemical *The Rise of Our East African Empire* (1893), Carl Peters's *New Light on Dark Africa* (1891), H. H. Johnston's *The Uganda Protectorate* (1902), Sir Charles Eliot's *The East African Protectorate* (1905), Von Lettow Vorbeck's *My Reminiscences of East Africa*, H. Schnee's *German Colonisation, Past and Future* (1926), Sir Frederick Jackson's inaccurate memoirs, *Early Days in East Africa* (1930) and Sir Donald Cameron's *My Tanganyika Service and Some Nigeria* (1938), in which the hand of the amateur author is plainly visible. In the missionary field, J. L. Krapf's *Travels, Researches and Missionary Labours in Eastern Africa* (1860), Tucker's *Eighteen Years in Uganda and East Africa* (1908), Bishop J. J. Willis's *An African Church in Building* (1925) and A. B. Cook's *Uganda Memories* (1945) might be cited as examples.

These pioneer efforts, especially those of missionaries

and administrators, later resulted in the founding of two omnibus journals in the 1930s which have contributed enormously towards the formation of the traditions of historical integrity in East Africa: *The Uganda Journal* and the *Tanganyika Notes and Records*, founded in 1933 and 1936 respectively with the official sponsorship, it is important to emphasize, of the colonial governments. *Tanganyika Notes and Records*, for example, was started through the initiative of Governor Sir Harold MacMichael. Much of the groundwork in the history of East Africa, especially in the histories of Uganda and Tanganyika, was done by amateurs, such as H. B. Thomas, who had gone out to Uganda as a surveyor before the First World War, and H. A. Fosbrooke in Tanganyika.

The greatest amateur of them all was Sir John Milner Gray, who went to Uganda in 1920 with some experience of historical research. No professional historian had as yet shown any interest in the history of East Africa. Gray soon acquired a knowledge of Luganda, and was thus the first to evaluate vernacular works, especially those of Sir Apolo Kagwa, *Basekabaka bya Buganda* (1901), *Mpisa za Buganda* (1905) and *Ebika bya Buganda* (1908). He also tapped French and German sources. And although he was transferred to Gambia before the first number of the *Uganda Journal* appeared, he contributed three significant articles to the first issues: 'Mutesa of Buganda', 'Early History of Buganda' and 'The Riddle of Biggo'.

He returned to East Africa in 1943 as Chief Justice of Zanzibar, and from this vantage point he became actively involved in exploring the whole field of East African history. As well as studying the Zanzibar Consular Archives, he also examined Arab, Portuguese and American sources for East African history. He distilled his findings into numerous articles which he published in both *The Uganda Journal* and *Tanganyika Notes and Records*. He also wrote several books: *Early Portuguese Missionaries in East Africa* (1958), *The British in Mombasa, 1824–1826* (1957), and a major work, *History of Zanzibar from the Middle Ages to 1856* (1962).[1]

The first professional historian to turn his attention to East Africa was Sir Reginald Coupland, who had succeeded H. E. Egerton as Beit Professor of Colonial History at Oxford. His special field was the British anti-slavery movement which, despite the existence of Adam Smith's *The Wealth of Nations*, he preferred to explain as a successful humanitarian crusade, a moral revolution. As Eric Williams has put it, 'Africa, slavery, and Britain's historical connection with it, became a virtual obsession with Coupland.'[2]

After publishing a biography of Wilberforce in 1923 and a brief study of the British anti-slavery movement in 1933, he turned his attention to East Africa, and gave us two books which are still standard works: *East Africa and its Invaders: From the Earliest Times to the Death of Seyyid Said in 1856* (1938) and *The Exploitation of East Africa, 1856–1890: The Slave Trade and the Scramble* (1939). In both of these works Coupland is obsessed with the abolition of the slave trade and Britain's noble role in it. In the first book, for instance, which is supposed to deal with the history of East Africa from the earliest times to 1856, Professor Coupland has little to say on the history of the African peoples, on two centuries of Portuguese rule in East Africa, and on Arab and Swahili settlements and culture at the coast. His main theme is the rise of the Omani rule in East Africa and the abolition of the slave trade by the British. He regrets that Nature had delayed the European occupation of the interior:

If the European occupation could have happened earlier and if—an essential condition—it could have been dissociated from the Slave Trade, the East Africans might likewise have begun earlier to emerge from their primitive life, to combat

---

[1] See 'Bibliography of the Works of Sir John Gray', *Tanganyika Notes and Records*, No. 53, 1959.

[2] Williams, E., *British Historians and the West Indies* (1966), p. 202.

more effectively their physical environment, to grow in prosperity and population. . . . More security for life and property,
better crops, better health, better education—those are the
ways in which the subjection of the East Africans has begun to
free them from the perilous, cramping, static conditions of a
tropical life secluded from all helpful contact with the rest of
the world.[3]

This theme—whether or not colonialism was an *essential
condition* for the development of East Africa—still dominates much of the historical writing in the region, as we
shall see later.

The other point which Coupland raised and which has
influenced East African historiography is that the history
of the region is essentially a history of its invaders. The
very title of his first book suggests this. And as a justifica-
tion he writes:

On nearly all, though not quite all, its pages, the history of
East Africa is only the history of its invaders. And the stage on
which they play their part is only a narrow slice of huge East
Africa. Not many miles back from their settlements and ports
and market-places a curtain falls shrouding the vast interior of
the continent in impenetrable darkness, 'where ignorant armies
clash by night'. But the reader should remember that the East
Africans, though invisible, are always there, a great black
background to the comings and goings of brown men and white
men on the coast. In the foreground, too, on the historical
stage itself, the East Africans are always the great majority,
dumb actors for the most part, doing nothing that seems important, so eclipsed by the protagonist that they are almost
forgotten, and yet quite indispensable.[4]

The emergence of university education in Africa ended
this romantic period of East African history. The first
history department in the region was built up by Professor
Kenneth Ingham at Makerere in Uganda, and this writer
was fortunate enough to be among his first students. Apart

[3] Coupland, R., *East Africa and its Invaders* (1938), pp. 13–14.
[4] Coupland, R., ibid, p. 14.

from his academic work, Ingham took an active part in public life as a backbench member of the Legislative Council. He and Antony Low, who since 1963 has been the Dean of the School of African and Asian Studies at the University of Sussex, realized that the proper subject-matter of an historical education in Africa must be African history. This led to an encouragement of serious research and a revaluation of the existing literary sources. Ingham himself wrote several books. In his *The Making of Modern Uganda* (1958), Ingham attempts to sketch the whole history of Uganda from the discovery of the area by the Europeans to the governorship of Sir Andrew Cohen. It is not a work of deep research, and it tells us little about the establishment of the Uganda Protectorate. His main aim, he says, was 'to trace the effects of British administration in Uganda'. The author relies heavily on official reports, and the whole book reads like an official history of Uganda.

Nor does Ingham's bigger and more important book, *A History of East Africa* (1962), which was sponsored by the then East Africa High Commission, show many signs of the revolution in African historiography. In a 456-page book which purports to deal with the history of East Africa from the earliest times to 1962, only twenty pages are allotted to the history of the interior of East Africa before the invaders as opposed to, for example, the thirteen pages on the well-worn stories of Krapf, Rebmann, Burton and Speke. This shows that we had not advanced very much beyond the age of Coupland.

Throughout the 1950s, more and more professional historians became interested in East African history, and most of them did a substantial part of their research in the region. But, on the whole, East African history was still conceived of in terms of invaders, as an aspect of the 'Expansion of Europe', although an increasing number of scholars were now becoming interested in the African response. Besides preoccupation with the invaders, the chief object of the historian of East Africa therefore became the impact of the external world upon the indigenous societies, and this is still the dominating theme. Most of the history books that have been published since 1952 deal with these two related themes: G. H. Mungeam's *British Rule in Kenya 1895–1912* (1966), which has been described by Professor Low as 'a very valuable resumé of the Foreign and Colonial Office dispatches'; J. F. Faupel's *African Holocaust: The Story of the Uganda Martyrs* (1962); G. Bennett's *Kenya: A Political History* (1963), which is really a story of European politics in Kenya; K. M. Stahl's *History of the Chagga People of Kilimanjaro* (1964), which says little about the Chagga origins or about relations with their neighbours; a whole catalogue of books on religion and society which start with Roland Oliver's pioneer study *The Missionary Factor in East Africa* (1952)—D. A. Low's *Religion and Society in Buganda, 1875–1900* (Kampala, 1957), F. B. Welbourn's *East African Rebels* (1961), J. V. Taylor's *The Growth of the Church in Buganda* (1958), H. P. Gale's *Uganda and the Mill Hill Fathers* (1959), F. B. Welbourn and B. A. Ogot's *A Place to Feel at Home* (1966) and J. S. Trimingham's *Islam in East Africa* (1964). In the economic field, we see the same engagement in the colonial debate in such books as C. C. Wrigley's *Crops and Wealth in Uganda* (Kampala, 1959), A. I. Richards' (ed.) *Economics, Development and Tribal Change* (1954), C. Ehrlich's *The Uganda Company Limited: The First Fifty Years* (Kampala, 1953) and Hugh Fearn's *An African Economy: A Study of the Economic Development of the Nyanza Province of Kenya, 1903–1953* (1961).

This obsession with East African invaders is seen in its most glaring form at the coast, where there is least cause for it. Despite a large crop of books which have recently been published on the East Coast, there are as yet no detailed studies of the coastal peoples. The coast has therefore been treated as an island isolated from the primitive interior, or as part of the Indian Ocean complex and therefore external to East Africa. C. R. Boxer and Carlos de

Azevedo's book *Fort Jesus and the Portuguese in Mombasa* (1960) is the story of the Portuguese in Mombasa, and corrects some of the points in Justus Strandes' classic *Die Portugiesenzeit von Deutsch- und Englisch-Ostafrika*, published in Berlin in 1899, and which has recently been translated from the German by Jean F. Wallwork with the title, *The Portuguese Period in East Africa* (Nairobi, 1961). Even Sir John Gray's important book *History of Zanzibar from the Middle Ages to 1856* (1962) is not free from this blemish. It is supposed to be a history of the two islands of Zanzibar and Pemba, yet one chapter is devoted to early times, two to the Portuguese period, one to the eighteenth century and *eight* to the reign of Seyyid Said. The first three chapters are superficial, and are not treated as part of a general history of the region as a whole. Seven of the eight chapters on Seyyid Said are concerned with the Sultan's relations with America, Portugal, France, Germany and England. Thus the main concern is with the invaders, in Coupland's tradition. There is only one chapter which discusses the relations between Said and the African inhabitants of Zanzibar and Pemba.

G. S. P. Freeman-Grenville's two books *The Medieval History of Tanganyika* (1962) and *The East African Coast: Select Documents from the First to the Earlier Nineteenth Century* (1962) also deal largely with invaders. The first book deals with early invaders, especially at Kilwa, and the second is a useful anthology of the principal written sources for the history of the coastal region, including the Swahili 'Chronicles'. But again these Greek, Arabic, Portuguese and Swahili texts deal largely with invaders. In all these works,[5] the East Africans remain 'dumb actors' or 'a great black background', and this is largely why no historical links have been discovered between the coast and its hinterland.

But reappraisal was not enough. Even when all the docu-

[5] For a detailed list see G. S. P. Freeman-Grenville, 'Historiography of the East African', *Tanganyika Notes and Records*, September 1960, No. 55.

mentary evidence had been fully exploited, large areas of East African history remained uncharted. There was the need to extend the field backwards in time and at the same time to put the African at the centre of such studies. New sources of evidence had to be tapped: oral traditions, archaeology, linguistics and social anthropology. African history had thus to depend increasingly on cooperation with other disciplines.

This new historiography was increasingly reflected in several of the articles that were contributed to *The Uganda Journal* and *Tanganyika Notes and Records*. In Uganda, for example, pioneer studies in the field of traditional history, such as Bishop J. Gorju's *Entre le Victoria, l'Albert et l'Edouard* (1920), and Sir Apolo Kagwa's three books already mentioned, were now supplemented by J. P. Crazzolara's three volumes on the *Lwoo* (Verona, 1950–4), A. G. Katate and L. Kamugungunu, *Abagabe b'Ankole* (2 volumes, Kampala, 1955) and J. W. Nyakatura's *Abakama ba Bunyoro-Kitara* (St Justine, Canada, 1947).

The first serious attempt to write the history of East Africa and not only that of its invaders was made in Volume I of the Oxford *History of East Africa* (1963), edited by Roland Oliver and Gervase Mathew. The book was the first of three volumes financed by Colonial Development and Welfare funds, and written mainly by British authors in the belief that: 'The publication of a comprehensive history of the region is one of the essential contributions which United Kingdom funds could make to the future of the new East African states.'[6] In other words this was to be part of Britain's *Uhuru* gift to the peoples of East Africa.

From the point of view of historiography, the most important fact was that for the first time a 500-page book was devoted to the pre-European history of East Africa. Professional historians had come to the aid of the amateurs by

[6] Roland Oliver and Gervase Mathew (eds.), *History of East Africa*, Vol. I (1963), p. v.

showing that it could be done, and by making sources such as oral evidence respectable.

But even this pioneer volume tells us little of what was happening inside the tribal societies, or of the inter-relations between them. And it is assumed, wrongly, throughout the book that the present consolidated tribal groupings in East Africa have been in existence for at least the last five hundred years, and that the work of the traditional historian is to write about these identifiable units. Moreover, eight out of the twelve chapters of the book really deal with conventional history whose main objective is still the impact of the outside world on the politics of the indigenous peoples.

Nor is it free from the colonial debate. The editors state in their introduction that 'To assess what the colonial period has done to the people of East Africa, it is more than ever necessary to know where they stood when it began.' In other words, Volume I of the Oxford *History of East Africa* was intended to provide a background against which British historians could assess their achievements in the two succeeding volumes.

Roland Oliver returns to this colonial debate in his Epilogue to the volume. He argues that the colonial period in East Africa provided the stimulus for social advance which, owing largely to the difficulties of porterage and communications in the pre-colonial technologies, could otherwise hardly have occurred. Colonialism, so the argument runs, led to the widening of the economic and political scales of the indigenous societies, and an enlargement of scale of this kind is essential for development.

For the integration of East Africa [he writes] with the general progress of mankind in the world outside, a drastic simplification of the old political diversity was an inescapable necessity. It was a problem which, judging by historical precedent, only a period of colonial tutelage could solve.[7]

This is true to the tradition of Coupland.

[7] *History of East Africa*, Vol. I, p. 456.

Since independence, East Africans have shown more interest in their pre-colonial history not as a background to a study of the European activities in Africa, but as an important aspect of human history which merits serious study in its own right. Detailed studies of pre-European East African polities such as this writer's *History of the Southern Luo*, Vol. I (Nairobi, 1966), G. S. Were's *History of the Abaluyia of Western Kenya* (Nairobi, 1967) and I. Kimambo's *Political History of the Pare* (Nairobi, 1969) have been published. The establishment of two other history departments at Nairobi and Dar es Salaam has stimulated much research activity in the region. Not only is the work on the pre-colonial period being extended to cover most parts of the region, but also a serious re-evaluation of the 'Colonial Reckoning' is being undertaken by the small but expanding school of East African scholars.

CHAPTER ELEVEN

Historians and Central Africa

Richard Gray

THE WORK of specialists from a wide variety of disciplines has recently been adding a new dimension to the historiography of Central Africa. As a result we can begin to trace a basic formative continuity, consisting of African initiatives, resilience and response, which extend back over the last two millennia. Take, for instance, the controversy and speculation which for more than a hundred years have surrounded Zimbabwe. Not surprisingly this site, by far the most impressive ancient monument in Africa south of the equator, has dominated work on the early history of Central Africa. Suggestions concerning the exotic identity of its builders have ranged from the Phoenicians to the Queen of Sheba; but in the last ten years the excavations of Roger Summers and Kenneth Robinson,[1] together with carbon dating, have fully confirmed the belief of earlier excavators, Randall MacIver and G. Caton-Thompson, that these stone buildings were the work of Iron Age Africans, and it is now possible to begin to set the history of this site into the broader framework of the whole area stretching from the Congo equatorial forest to the Transvaal.

Zimbabwe's origins probably go back to the very early history of the Bantu expansion. Here some of the most significant recent work has been done not by an archaeologist but by a linguist. After a scrutiny, lasting more than

[1] Usefully summarized in Roger Summers, *Zimbabwe. A Rhodesian Mystery* (1963).

twenty-five years, of the distribution of common Bantu cognates, Malcolm Guthrie has concluded that the parent language, from which have descended the Bantu languages spoken over nearly the whole of Africa south of the equator, must have been developed in a nuclear area situated in the savannah belt south of the Congo forest.[2] Roland Oliver has suggested that iron technology coupled with agricultural skills may have supplied the momentum to enable these Bantu-speakers to expand rapidly outwards from this nuclear centre,[3] and although, until much more archaeological work has been done, this line of thought must remain speculative, it seems at present reasonable to suggest that the first Iron Age agriculturalists, whose pottery is found at the lowest levels at Zimbabwe, may well have been closely related to the first Bantu-speakers to have settled south of the Zambesi.

Subsequently, from probably about the fourth to the eleventh century, Zimbabwe was occupied by people with a different pottery tradition. Their fairly simple material culture was similar to that of their contemporaries over much of Central Africa. These people, to judge from two well-known examples, the Leopard's Kopje culture in Rhodesia and the Kalomo culture in southern Zambia, were pastoralists as well as agriculturalists. The small cattle figurines found at Zimbabwe from this period may, therefore, record a very early stage of the great pastoral traditions of Southern Africa. Through the growing of crops and the herding of cattle, these Africans of the first millennium A.D. had thus begun to exploit the agricultural potential of their environment and, despite subsequent shocks and invasions, their descendants have continued to occupy a large part of this ancestral heritage. In this early twilight we can therefore already glimpse one of the basic components of the area's subsequent history.

[2] Professor Guthrie has summarized his argument in an article in *Journal of African History*, Vol. III, No. 2 (1962).

[3] See his article in *Journal of African History*, Vol. VII, No. 3 (1966).

Period III at Zimbabwe, with the beginning of stone-building in about the eleventh century and with a marked increase in the richness and variety of imported trade goods, may seem at first sight to mark a break in this pattern of African development and initiative. In this period gold from the Rhodesian plateau was the mainstay of the Arabs' Indian Ocean trade, providing the economic foundation for the growth of medieval Kilwa and for the rich Islamic culture of the East African coast. Is it, one might ask, a mere coincidence that the great buildings of Zimbabwe are found at the point in the African interior in closest contact with this flourishing trade? Did these African builders derive their cultural stimulus and inspiration from contact with the outside world? Some recent writings have stressed the Arab role at Zimbabwe and in the fifteenth-century empire of Mwene Mutapa, and at first sight this line of speculation would seem to be strengthened by Brian Fagan's excavations at Ingombe Ilede.[4] Here right up the Zambesi, near the modern Kariba Dam, burials from the fourteenth and fifteenth centuries have yielded a wide range of alien trade goods, together with some of the finest Iron Age pottery from Central or Southern Africa. Even more significant, however, is the impressive evidence of those indigenous industrial skills —cloth-weaving and a most sophisticated metallurgy— which are also the hallmarks of the Zimbabwe culture at its greatest. Before concluding, however, that here again this rich cultural development is merely the reflection in the African interior of an alien commercial stimulus, one must consider the evidence from a third major site in Central Africa.

In the heart of Bantu Africa, at Lake Kisale in the Katanga, two extensive Iron Age cemeteries, excavated by Jacques Nenquin, have provided abundant evidence of similar, specialized industrial skills, in the manufacture of

[4] See his chapter in J. D. Fage and Roland Oliver, *Papers in African Prehistory* (1969).

copper and iron artifacts demanding an extraordinary precision and technical mastery comparable to the finest work at Zimbabwe or Ingombe Ilede. But here the total exotic imports found with the Kisalian burials amounted to four opaque glass beads and one cowrie shell, and the typical Kisalian pottery has a carbon date of 720 A.D. $\pm$ 120. Thus long before period III at Zimbabwe, and long before the trading centre at Ingombe Ilede, Africans, deep in the interior and apparently completely isolated from direct external contact, had already moved far beyond the simple skills of the early Iron Age. Already in the basic industrial crafts they had accomplished a technological advance which sharply distinguished their way of life, together with that of period III Zimbabwe, or its sister site of Mapungubwe, south of the Limpopo, from the simpler cultures of the early Iron Age. The granite kopjes of Zimbabwe and the Rhodesian plateau were to provide abundant building materials which enabled its occupants to construct the monuments which still astonish us, but if for a moment we lift our eyes off the buildings and the exotic, oriental imports, the crucial, distinctive tradition of sophisticated industrial skills leads us indisputably back to Negro Africa.

Archaeological discoveries are therefore directing our attention away from alien influences to the energies generated within Africa itself. Similarly, work on oral traditions is beginning to recapture a continuity of African initiative. Donald Abraham's study of Shona traditions suggests that it may well prove possible to establish clear and close links between the archaeological evidence and the dynastic memories of still extant groups, and he has already thrown much light on the political role of early religious cults, including those connected with Zimbabwe.[5] Equally it is now obvious that the Portuguese destruction of the Arab gold trade from Sofala and the Zambesi in the sixteenth century did not result in a sharp break and a

[5] See his chapter in J. Vansina, R. Mauny and L. V. Thomas, *The Historian in Tropical Africa* (1964), and other references given there.

disastrous and uniform decline throughout Central Africa. Admittedly Portuguese penetration in the Zambesi valley reduced the famous Mwene Mutapa dynasty to a mere shadow of its former self. Some of the details of this story have been ably examined by Eric Axelson from the wide range of Portuguese sources; further light has been thrown on Portuguese activities by Portuguese historians, notably by Alexandre Lobato and Caetano Montez, and by the continued publication of contemporary Portuguese documents.[6] But Malyn Newitt's recent thesis on the Portuguese prazos in the Zambesi valley shows that, even in this area of close contact with the alien intruders, it was the African, and not the European, culture which proved the stronger, so that by the nineteenth century the prazo owners had become tribal chiefs leading an African resistance to renewed European pressures.[7]

Beyond this restricted arena of direct encounter with the Portuguese, African initiative continued to be of untrammelled significance. After expelling the Portuguese from their fairs along the escarpment of the Zambesi valley at the end of the seventeenth century, the Rozwi *Mambos*, overlords of most of the Shona kingdoms, successfully prevented the Portuguese from gaining access to the gold-mining regions south of the Zambesi. Controlling the major supplies of gold, the Rozwi were able to insist that the Portuguese traded with them only through African intermediaries. Isolated thus from any direct external pressure, they enriched the culture and technological achievements which they inherited from the earlier inhabitants of Zimbabwe. Both in contemporary Portuguese documents and in their ruined sites, particularly those of Khami and Dhlo Dhlo, their peace and prosperity can be traced, until in the nineteenth century the Ngoni and Ndebele invasions sud-

---

[6] See Eric Axelson, *South-East Africa, 1488–1530* (1940) and *The Portuguese in South-East Africa, 1600–1700* (1960), in the latter of which references are given to the other material mentioned.

[7] See his article in *Journal of African History*, Vol. X, No. 1 (1969).

denly exposed them to the aftermath of the Zulu military revolution, soon to be followed by European conquest and settlement.

North of the Zambesi ivory, rather than gold, was the main export commodity. Here Edward Alpers has recently revealed a fascinating picture of African commercial initiative.[8] From the sixteenth century onwards the peoples of the north bank, the Maravi, Zimba and Yao, reacted to the Portuguese presence on the Zambesi by rapidly constructing an overland trading network, which enabled these African traders, right into the nineteenth century, to dominate the vast commercial hinterland of Kilwa and Moçambique island by skilfully exploiting French, Portuguese and Arab rivalries on the coast. Here then the initiative came from the interior, and the fortunes of coastal ports depended in part on the decisions taken by these African entrepreneurs operating around Lake Malawi. By the eighteenth century these trading links had been extended westwards by the Bisa, Lenje and other Zambian peoples to connect, through Kazembe's Lunda, with the commercial network based on the Atlantic coast, whence the tentacles of the slave trade had driven deep into the interior. The inter-relationship of trade and politics throughout this vast, trans-continental area south of the Congo forest is obviously one of the major arenas for future research. Already, however, David Birmingham's study of the commercial and political conflict between the Mbundu and the Portuguese in Angola, together with Jan Vansina's wide-ranging survey of the savannah kingdoms, have indicated the exciting possibilities of this theme, and two important pieces of research supervised by Vansina—those of Andrew Roberts on the Bemba and Joseph Miller on the Cokwe—have illustrated it still further.[9]

[8] See, for example, his article in *Journal of African History*, Vol. X, No. 3 (1969).

[9] David Birmingham, *Trade and Conflict in Angola, 1483–1790* (1966); Jan Vansina, *Kingdoms of the Savanna* (1966).

In the nineteenth and twentieth centuries, European activities manifestly constitute a theme of considerable, and at moments of overwhelming, significance in the history of Central Africa. This development has indeed attracted its fair measure of attention, notably with Lewis Gann's documented, scholarly studies on Zambia and Rhodesia.[10] The very wealth of European documentation tends, however, to obscure and distort the African role during this period. We have almost certainly overestimated the break caused by alien domination, and historians have only recently begun to pierce beyond the reports of European observers into the continuities of African responses and reactions. George Shepperson and Thomas Price pioneered the way with their study of John Chilembwe, the independent Christian leader whose revolt in Malawi during the First World War exemplifies one major strand in early African nationalism.[11] More recently Terence Ranger's book on the Ndebele and Shona rebellions has shown how the religious cults, associated for centuries with Zimbabwe and the Shona kingdoms, survived the impact of the Ndebele conquest to animate and direct one of the fiercest African resistances to the imposition of European rule, a resistance which finds its contemporary echoes as modern African nationalists adopt Zimbabwe as their symbol and inspiration.[12] As other scholars, and especially the rising generation of African historians, follow in the footsteps of these pioneer investigators, and as they exploit the African as well as the European sources, it should become increasingly easier to glimpse the threads of the long, seamless web of Central African history, and to evaluate more clearly the interactions of those peoples for whom this vast and varied area constitutes home.

[10] Lewis Gann, *A History of Northern Rhodesia* (1964); *A History of Southern Rhodesia* (1965).
[11] *Independent African* (1958).
[12] *Revolt in Southern Rhodesia, 1896–1897* (1967).

CHAPTER TWELVE

Historians and South Africa

Shula Marks

IT IS A curious irony that while probably more has been
written about South Africa than about any other country
in Africa, very little has been written by historians of South
Africa about the history of the majority of its population.
In the past ten or fifteen years our conception of African
history has been radically revised. The earlier view that
before the coming of the white man Africa was not only
the Black Continent but also, historically speaking, 'the
Blank Continent', has been so clearly shown to be invalid
that there is no need here to labour the point.

Through the combined use of oral tradition, archaeology, linguistic and anthropological evidence, our knowledge of the African past has been pushed back well into
pre-literate times. For the pre-colonial period, early and
scanty references to Africa by her earliest literate visitors
have been re-interpreted and given new relevance when
combined with oral tradition. And the historian of the
colonial period is increasingly realizing the limitations of
a view based solely on the documented evidence of policy-
makers and rulers.

For a number of reasons, however, this change in think-
ing has stopped short at the Limpopo River, South Africa's
northern boundary; the new approach to African history
has found no echo in the history being written and taught
in South Africa. In part, of course, this is explicable in
purely political terms. It is no coincidence that the revision
in African historiography came with the end of the colonial

period and the advent of independence in tropical Africa. In Southern Africa European rule has not yet come to an end.

Some five or ten years ago Rhodesia had a flourishing school of history, where significant advances were being made in writing the history of all the peoples of the territory through the fruitful collaboration of archaeologists, ethno-historians, historians and anthropologists. Today that school is virtually dead, and few professional historians are left in Rhodesia. For someone with his interests primarily in African as opposed to settler history, it is clearly difficult to live in the political, social and emotional climate of Salisbury.

In the Republic of South Africa, the situation is even more complex. As in Rhodesia, the regime is not sympathetic to the freedom of intellectual activity in general, nor the writing of African history in particular. Thus one of the recurrent myths of South African history is that by a curious, if irrelevant, coincidence, the black man first crossed the Limpopo River in the north at the same time as the first Dutch settlers arrived at the Cape in the south. Not only does this myth ignore all the archaeological evidence and, indeed, even documentary evidence—such as the accounts of shipwrecked Portuguese sailors—to the contrary; by ignoring their existence, it also turns the earlier inhabitants whom the Dutch encountered at the Cape into a kind of non-people. This myth is repeated not only in all government propaganda on the subject, but also in all school history books.

The whole of South African history is subject to similar distortions. For the vast majority of white South African school children, the Africans are still savages who treacherously massacred their pioneering ancestors. Few if any of them have heard of the impressive Iron Age sites associated with Bantu-speakers in Southern Africa, such as Zimbabwe or Mapungubwe. Not surprisingly therefore, for most South Africans the history of their country is the history of inter-white politics, and even this lacks objectivity.

In South Africa, as nowhere else in Africa, there is a large white minority which can trace its own historical roots in the continent back to the seventeenth century. To the political scientist, the student of race relations and the contemporary historian, it has generally seemed that the top priority must be to trace the evolution of this group, its adaptation to the South African environment and its eventual accession to power. History tends to record the activities of the successful—and in the context of the immediate present it is the nationalism of the white Afrikaners that is triumphantly successful.

In general, South African historiography to date has reflected the racial and political divisions in the country. Afrikaans-speaking South Africans are still intensely absorbed in their own exclusive national past. Afrikaner historiography centres on the evolution of Afrikaner nationalism and the formative episodes in this evolution: the highly romanticized pioneering saga of the Great Trek, the first Transvaal War of Independence in 1881, and the South African War of 1899–1902. The spirit of much of this history can be summed up in the title of a pamphlet written during the latter war: *A Century of Wrong*. And the 'wrongs' done the Afrikaners were firstly by the British, and secondly by the Africans. However, even within the rather limited framework of Afrikaner history, not all themes have proved attractive to the Afrikaner historian: the Afrikaner Bond, for example—the chief political and nationalist organization of Afrikaners in the Cape until 1910—has had to find its historian in an English-speaking scholar, Dr Rodney Davenport.[1]

Afrikaner nationalist historians have had their counterpart among English-speaking historians in the 'jingo' school of history, namely those writers who have defended every action of the imperial power against both the Afrikaners and the Africans. Although there are few historians writing in this extreme tradition today, some of the

[1] *The Afrikaner Bond* (1966).

attitudes are still revealed among those historians and critics in Britain who attribute the present situation in South Africa to peculiar vices of the Afrikaner. If only English-speaking South Africans had won political control after the South African War, a book reviewer in the *Times Literary Supplement* suggested recently, there would have been no *apartheid* in South Africa today. The role of English-speaking Natal in formulating and rationalizing many of the theories and practices of present-day *apartheid* passes unnoticed in this judgment, as does the more liberal attitude of many Afrikaners in the Western Cape at the turn of the century.

Probably the most important school of history in South Africa until very recently, and certainly the one that has been closest to the historical tradition of the West, has consisted of predominantly English-speaking 'liberal' historians, such as C. W. de Kiewiet, W. M. Macmillan, J. S. Marais and L. M. Thompson. (It is noteworthy that only Marais still lives in South Africa.) Undoubtedly the contribution they have made to historical studies in South Africa has been immense.[2] Nevertheless, the very label 'liberal' suggests some of their preoccupations. Deeply concerned by the racial antagonism in South Africa, they were mainly interested in the evolution of race attitudes in the nineteenth century, and in the closely related twin problems of land and labour.

By and large they were less keenly aware of the problems of urbanization and industrialization, or of the part of African history that happened either before the advent of the white man or out of his immediate presence. They tended to underestimate the vitality of African life, and its surprising elasticity even in the face of considerable onslaughts from the settler administration. The processes of

---

[2] For example: C. W. de Kiewiet, *A History of South Africa: Social and Economic* (1941); W. M. Macmillan, *Bantu, Boer and Briton* (1929); J. S. Marais, *The Cape Coloured People* (1939); L. M. Thompson, *The Unification of South Africa 1902–1910* (1960).

African state-building in the early part of the nineteenth century were largely outside their ken, as have been rebellions and resistance to colonial rule. Thus, for example, the great upheavals associated with the rise of the Zulu kingdom, which have rightly been called a formative and revolutionary event in African history, have only just received attention in Professor Omer-Cooper's *Zulu Aftermath*.

In the past it was understandable that the historian with a strongly developed social conscience should have regarded race relations as his first priority. That today liberal historians in South Africa do not see that there is an African past prior to the coming of the white man, or an African history apart from the interaction between the groups, reveals only too starkly the white-centred nature of South African historiography, and the growing isolation of South African historians from new work being done in the African field.

In so far as attempts have been made to penetrate the African past, they have been made by anthropologists. Probably the most outstanding of these is Professor Monica Wilson of the University of Cape Town, whose article 'The Early History of the Transkei and Ciskei' was a fine example of what can be done by combining oral tradition, archaeology and documentary evidence.[3] It has been emulated by very few historians in South Africa.

Why then, it may be asked, do not Africans write their own history as they are doing in the rest of the continent? Why is it that while South Africa has produced outstanding African musicians and writers, as well as doctors, lawyers and teachers, there has been no outstanding African historian as yet? Africans have written histories both in the vernacular and in English, and a number of articles in the vernacular press have real historical value. However these have generally been of limited scope and of essentially local significance.

[3] See also her contributions to Monica Wilson and L. M. Thompson, *The Oxford History of South Africa*, Vol. I (1969).

Some of the more recent African historical writing however has shared the faults of extreme Afrikaner nationalist historiography. Africans also want to describe their 'Century of Wrong'. For an articulate, historically conscious African to stand aside from the present political struggle would require almost superhuman effort.

Moreover, whereas in the rest of Africa Africans are now taking a renewed interest in their tribal origins, in South Africa this approach is still slightly suspect. To return to the traditions of the past has smacked too much of the government's explicit aim of reviving tribalism, and its fostering of eight separate 'Bantu nationalities' or ethnic 'Bantustans'. The aim of African nationalists in South Africa has always been to inculcate a pan-South African nationalism and to overcome tribal particularism. It remains to be seen whether the government policy of Bantustans, and an educational system which ostensibly encourages tribal values and a return to the vernacular, will not lead also to a revival of traditional histories. These may have a value and a significance unsuspected by the white politicians who rule the Republic.

In the case of South Africa, therefore, the responsibility for exploring the history of African peoples falls heavily on those scholars working outside the Republic. At both the School of Oriental and African Studies in London and at the University of California at Los Angeles, a small number of young historians, not all of them expatriates, are trying to see South African history in its African context, for the first time. So far most of them are working on nineteenth-century themes.

In sharp contrast to the situation just slightly further north, in Rhodesia and Zambia, very little Iron Age archaeology has been done in South Africa, though a certain amount of work has been done in the central and southern Transvaal. The lack of detailed historico-linguistic analyses also makes it difficult for the student outside South Africa to make much headway in the very early period of African history. Nor has much work been done as yet on the possibility of using the extensive Dutch material to explore the history of African people, whether Khoikhoi- or Bantu-speaking, in the seventeenth and eighteenth centuries. It may be that through using Dutch sources together with the oral traditions, some of them recorded very early on in the nineteenth century, much of Xhosa and Southern Tswana history from the early eighteenth, if not the late seventeenth century, could be recovered.

For the nineteenth century, both subjects and material are so abundant that they almost constitute an embarrass-ment of riches. From the last quarter of the eighteenth century the records of explorers become voluminous, and are added to by the journals of traders and missionaries. With the expansion of white settlement and the extension of European administration, the documentary material becomes comparable with that for any other field of his-tory. Although it can be argued that administrative records do not always reflect what was happening amongst the African population, in the earlier period the writings of missionaries, and increasingly, later on, those of literate Africans, especially in the vernacular press, enable the bias to be in large measure corrected.

If this essay has been a plea for the writing of the black man's history in South Africa, it is only because up to now the historical balance has been so heavily tilted in favour of white South Africans. Only the most prejudiced would not agree that the history of South Africa must be the his-tory of all her peoples, Afrikaners as well as Africans, earliest inhabitants like the Khoikhoi (Hottentots) and Saan (Bushmen), as well as later arrivals such as the English-speaking and Asian immigrants of the nineteenth century. It is the very complexity and multiplicity of the strands that make its writing a worthwhile and challenging occupation.

Index